PRACTICAL ART

OILS

A STEP-BY-STEP GUIDE TO OIL TECHNIQUES

PRACTICAL ART

OILS

A STEP-BY-STEP GUIDE TO OIL TECHNIQUES

ANGELA GAIR

TIGER BOOKS
INTERNATIONAL
LONDON

First published in 1997 by
New Holland (Publishers) Ltd
London • Cape Town • Sydney • Singapore

24 Nutford Place
London W1H 6DQ
United Kingdom

80 McKenzie Street
Cape Town 8001
South Africa

3/2 Aquatic Drive
Frenchs Forest, NSW 2086
Australia

This edition published in 1997 by Tiger Books International Plc, Twickenham

ISBN 1 85501 869 1

Designed and edited by
Axis Design
311 Regents Park Road
London N3 1DP

Editor: Phyllis Richardson
Designer: Sian Keogh
Photographer: Chas Wilder

Reproduction by P & W, Singapore
Printed and bound in Malaysia by Times Offset (M) Sdn Bhd

ACKNOWLEDGEMENTS
Special thanks are due to Daler-Rowney, P.O. Box 10, Bracknell,
Berkshire, RG12 4ST, for providing the materials and equipment featured in this book.

CONTENTS

INTRODUCTION 7

MATERIALS AND EQUIPMENT 10

BASIC TECHNIQUES 16

GALLERY 21

TECHNIQUES

1 PAINTING "ALLA PRIMA" 27

2 IMPASTO 33

3 USING A TONED GROUND 39

4 WORKING "FAT OVER LEAN" 45

5 EXPRESSIVE BRUSHWORK 53

6 SCUMBLING 61

7 DEVELOPING THE PAINTING 69

8 KNIFE PAINTING 75

9 BLENDING 83

10 UNDERPAINTING 89

SUPPLIERS 95

INDEX 96

INTRODUCTION

The Flemish painter Jan van Eyck (c.1390–1441) has been called the inventor of oil painting. Although this is not strictly true – various oils had been used as paint mediums since the twelfth century – his discoveries and techniques certainly laid the foundations for the art.

Before Van Eyck's innovations, artists painted on wooden panels with egg tempera, which was a difficult medium to use as it dried very fast and thus called for a deliberate and meticulous approach. Around 1420, when van Eyck found that one of his tempera paintings had split while drying in the sun, he determined to "devise means for preparing a kind of varnish which should dry in the shade, so as to avoid having to place the pictures in the sun".

He experimented with raw pigments bound with linseed and nut oils, and found that they dried in the shade to form a hard film without cracking. He also discovered, to his delight, that the oil binder rendered the pigments translucent, at the same time giving them a richly saturated appearance. When applied in thin, transparent layers, the colours took on a depth and luminosity hitherto unknown. Furthermore, the glossy consistency and slow drying of oil paints meant that painters could work more freely than with tempera, applying colours in broad areas and blending tones on the support itself.

Self-portrait at the Easel *Rembrandt van Rijn*

Rembrandt's technical mastery of the oil medium and his profound insight into the human spirit are marvellously combined in this self-portrait. A suggestiveness of mood is created by his use of chiaroscuro (strong contrasts of light and shadow).

The Arnolfini Marriage *Jan van Eyck*

This tender portrait of a couple plighting their troth is rich in symbolism. The candle flames are emblematic of the ardour of newlyweds; the dog is a symbol of marital faith; and the figure carved on the back of the chair is St Margaret, patron saint of childbirth. Each object is lovingly described with a subtlety and refinement that the oil medium allowed for the first time.

Nevertheless, the early painters in oil, including van Eyck, painted in a style that looks carefully detailed when compared to the freedom of handling that modern painters enjoy. To produce highly polished and realistic paintings, the paint was laid on thinly in flat, separate areas and brushed to produce a smooth satin finish with delicate brushstrokes that are almost invisible to the eye.

The full potential of oil paint was not really exploited until it was taken up by Titian (1490–1576) and other Italian painters of the fifteenth and sixteenth centuries. The breadth of handling in Titian's later paintings at last revealed the medium's hitherto unleashed powers of expression. He laid in the picture lightly in monochrome, then combined delicately painted areas of glazing (thin paint applied in transparent layers over one another) with thick brushstrokes in which the actual marks of the brush became a feature rather than something to be disguised.

This fluency of technique was developed further by the Flemish painter Peter Paul Rubens (1577–1640). On a trip to Venice he studied the works of Titian, who became a lifelong inspiration. Rubens' innovation was to work on a brown priming brushed on with long, irregular strokes that allowed the white chalk ground to shine through and illuminate the succeeding colours. He also abandoned the practice of making a detailed underdrawing before beginning to paint, and reversed the normal painting procedure: working from thin darks to thickly applied lights with fluid, vigorous brushwork. At times Rubens' compositions transmit such dynamic energy that it is difficult to believe they are mere two-dimensional representations.

The Spanish painter Diego Velázquez (1599–1660) was another artist who was greatly ahead of his time. His later work demonstrates the influence of Titian as well as his friend Rubens, and around 1627 he abandoned his chiaroscuro style for an effect that would later become associated with Impressionism. The open, painterly quality of his brushwork and his portrayal of the shimmering qualities of light appears to anticipate the work of Monet.

Hélèna Fourment with a Carriage *Peter Paul Rubens*

Rubens painted many portraits of his second wife. In this one Hélèna is seen as a young woman of fashion. The painter's sure touch conveys the various textures of her gown, from the heavy satin skirt to the gauzy veil.

The influence of Rubens can be traced through generations of painters, including the greatest of all paint handlers, Rembrandt (1606–69). Never before had a painter taken such a purely sensuous delight in the physical qualities of his medium. Rembrandt worked in complex layers, building up translucent glazes and rich impastos that were astounding. In seeking to suggest textures, such as the wrinkled skin of an old face, or the frothy white lace of a collar, he bent the medium to his will, rubbing, scrubbing and dabbing the paint to create a rich, broken surface.

By the end of the eighteenth century many artists began to reject the staid conventions of traditional oil painting, and the methodical working up of a picture in layers was challenged and replaced by new, more direct techniques in which the artist laid on each patch of colour more or less as it was finally intended to appear. The freshness of this technique can be seen in the works of John Constable (1776–1837) and JMW Turner (1775–1851), whose works were painted directly from nature. A stimulus was given to this spontaneous approach by the introduction of

Grain Stacks, End of Summer *Claude Monet*

Between 1889 and 1891 Monet completed a series of over 30 paintings of grain stacks in the field behind his house. Each study captures a brief moment in nature, and Monet worked on several canvases concurrently, dashing from one to the other as the light changed.

collapsible tin tubes of paint in the mid-nineteenth century. This was a boon to landscape painters, for it enabled them to take their paints outside and work immediately in front of nature. Hitherto, oil painting had been largely a studio activity as pigment had to be ground by hand and used instantly.

The biggest revolution in oil painting came in the 1860s and 1870s with the French Impressionists, who perhaps have had the greatest impact on the way that artists approach oil painting today. Monet (1840–1926), Renoir (1841– 1919), Pissarro (1831–1903) and others tried to capture in their paintings the many moods and qualities of light and colour in the landscape as they experienced them directly in the open air.

The Impressionists applied a broken-colour technique in which thick strokes and dabs of opaque colour were laid down separately, side by side, so that they mixed not on the canvas but in the viewer's eye. Rather than a solid, carefully built-up surface, the eye perceives a mosaic of fragmented brushstrokes that only forms a vibrant whole when viewed from a distance.

The Impressionist legacy has spawned a proliferation of art movements during the twentieth century, and artists have felt free to work in whatever way they wish. At one extreme, surrealist painters such as Salvador Dali (1904–1989) used traditional techniques in order to produce a kind of photographic realism. At the other extreme, artists such as the American abstract expressionist Jackson Pollock (1912–1956) have extended the boundaries of oil painting by throwing paint onto the canvas and allowing it to drip.

Despite the arrival of new media such as acrylic and alkyd paints, oil paint has lost none of its attraction – rather, its possibilities have increased beyond anything that could have been imagined by previous masters of the medium.

MATERIALS AND EQUIPMENT

M aterials for oil painting can be expensive, therefore it is advisable to start out with the essentials and add extra colours, brushes and so on as you gain more experience.

PAINTS

Oil paints are sold in tubes and are available in two different grades: artists' and students'. Artists' colours are of better quality and this is reflected in the price. They are made from the finest pigments ground with a minimum of oil so their consistency is stiff, and the colours retain their brilliance well.

Students' colours are labelled with trade names such as "Georgian" (Daler-Rowney) or "Winton" (Winsor & Newton). These paints cost less because they contain less pure pigment and more fillers and extenders. They cannot provide the same intensity of colour as the artists' range. They are, however, fine for practising with. Some artists even combine the two types, using artists' paints for the pure, intense colours and students' paints for the earth colours, which are often just as good as those in the artists' range.

Artist-quality paints vary in price according to the initial cost of the pigment. They are classified according to a "series", typically from 1 (the cheapest) to 7 (the most costly). Student colours are sold at a uniform price.

Oil paint consists of dry pigments ground in a natural drying oil, such as linseed or safflower oil.

MEDIUMS AND DILUENTS

Oil paint can be used thickly, direct from the tube, but usually it needs to be diluted to make it easier to apply. Paint may be thinned to the required consistency with a diluent such as distilled turpentine or white spirit, or a combination of a diluent and an oil or varnish – what artists call a *medium*.

Diluents

Paint mixed with a diluent alone dries quickly to a matt finish. Always use double-distilled or rectified turpentine – ordinary household turpentine contains too many impurities. If you find that it gives you a headache or irritates your skin, white spirit is a suitable alternative.

Even small quantities of solvents and thinners can be hazardous if not used with care, because their fumes are rapidly absorbed through the lungs.

SUGGESTED PALETTE

Cobalt Blue
Greener and paler than ultramarine blue, cobalt is good for skies and cool highlights in flesh tones.

Lemon Yellow
A transparent colour with a cool, pale yellow hue. It forms delicate, cool greens when mixed with blues.

French Ultramarine
This is the best general-purpose blue. A deep, warm blue, it mixes well with yellow to form a rich variety of greens and with earth colours to form colourful greys.

Cadmium Yellow
A bright, warm yellow with good covering power.

Cadmium Red
A warm, intense red. Produces good pinks and purples when mixed with blues.

Viridian
A bright, deep green with a bluish tinge. When squeezed from the tube it appears a "synthetic" green, but is wonderful in mixes.

Titanium White
A good, dense white that mixes well and has excellent covering power.

Cobalt Violet
Though you can make a violet with red and blue, it won't have the intensity of cobalt violet. A very expensive pigment, however.

Raw Sienna
A warm, transparent colour, very soft and subtle. Useful in landscapes.

Permanent Rose
A cool, pinkish red that is similar to alizarin crimson but not quite so overpowering in mixes. It is good for mixing pinks and purples.

Burnt Sienna
A rich, reddish-brown hue, useful for warming other colours. Mix it with ultramarine or viridian to make deep, rich dark tones.

Burnt Umber
A rich, opaque and versatile brown. Useful for darkening all colours.

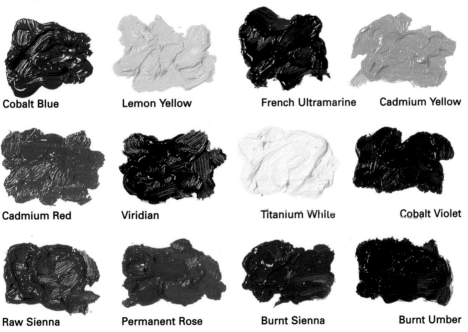

Cobalt Blue | Lemon Yellow | French Ultramarine | Cadmium Yellow

Cadmium Red | Viridian | Titanium White | Cobalt Violet

Raw Sienna | Permanent Rose | Burnt Sienna | Burnt Umber

rag

oil paint (225ml size)

tear-off
paper
palette

mahl stick

turpentine

linseed oil

oblong
palettes

dammar
varnish

single
dipper

artist-grade
oil paint
(38ml size)

synthetic brushes

fan
brush

studio
palette

flat

filbert

round

sable brush

double
dipper

household
decorating brush

painting
knives

palette
knife

gesso
primer

texture
paste

student-grade
oil paint
(38ml size)

picture
varnish

rabbit-skin
size

stretcher
bars

hog bristle brushes

wooden
keys

varnishing
brush

When using solvents, always work in a well-ventilated room and avoid inhalation. Do not eat, drink or smoke while working.

Mediums

Various oils and resins can be mixed with a diluent to add texture and body to the paint. The most commonly used medium is a mixture of linseed oil and turpentine, usually in a ratio of 60% oil to 40% turpentine. Linseed oil dries to a glossy finish that is resistant to cracking – but be sure to buy either purified or cold-pressed linseed oil; boiled linseed oil contains impurities that cause rapid yellowing. Adding a little dammar varnish to the turpentine and linseed oil produces a thicker mixture that dries more quickly.

Ready-mixed painting mediums are available, designed variously to improve the flow of the paint, thicken it for impasto work, speed its drying rate, and produce a matt or a gloss finish.

BRUSHES

Oil-painting brushes come in a range of sizes and shapes. Each makes a different kind of mark, but some are more versatile than others.

Bristle brushes

Stiff and hard-wearing, bristle brushes are good for moving the paint around on the surface and for applying thick dabs of colour. The best ones are made of stiff, white hog bristles with split ends that hold a lot of paint.

Sable brushes

Sable brushes are soft and springy, similar to those used for watercolours, but with longer handles. They are useful for adding details in the final layers of a painting and for applying thinly diluted colour.

Synthetic brushes

These are an economical alternative to natural-hair brushes, and their quality has improved considerably in recent years. They are hard-wearing and easily cleaned.

Brush shapes

Rounds have long, thin bristles that curve inwards at the ends. This is the most versatile brush shape as it covers large areas quickly and is also good for sketching in outlines.

Flats have square ends. They are ideal for applying thick, bold colour and for blending. Use the square end for fine lines and sharp details. So-called "long flats" have longer bristles that hold a lot of paint.

Brights are the same shape as flats, but with shorter, stiffer bristles that make very textured strokes. The stiff bristles are used to apply thick, heavy paint to produce impasto effects.

Filberts are similar to flats, except that the bristles curve inwards at the end. They produce a range of marks. The curved tip is useful for softening and blending edges.

Fan blenders are available in hog bristle, sable and synthetic fibre, and are used for blending colours where a very smooth, highly finished effect is required.

Sizes

Each type of brush comes in a range of sizes, from 00 to around 16. Brush sizes are not standardized and can vary widely between brands. The size you choose will depend on the scale and style of your paintings. In general, it is better to start with medium to large brushes as they cover large areas quickly but can also be employed for small touches. Using bigger brushes also encourages a more painterly, generous approach.

Almost any surface is suitable for oil painting so long as it is properly prepared.

PALETTES

Palettes come in a variety of shapes, sizes and materials. The best-quality palettes are made of mahogany ply, but fibreboard and melamine-faced palettes are adequate.

Thumbhole palettes

Thumbhole palettes come in various sizes and are designed to be held while painting at the easel. They have a thumbhole and indentation for the fingers, and the palette is supported on the forearm. There are three main shapes: oblong, oval and the traditional kidney-shaped, or "studio" palette. For easel painting, the curved shape of the studio palette is the best choice as it is well balanced and comfortable to hold for long periods.

Disposable palettes

Made of oil-proof paper, disposable palettes are useful for outdoor work and for artists who hate cleaning up. They come in pads with tear-off sheets.

Improvised palettes

Any smooth, non-porous material is suitable, such as a sheet of white formica, a glass slab with white or neutral-coloured paper underneath, or a sheet of hardboard sealed with a coat of paint.

SUPPORTS

Supports for oil painting – whether canvas, board or paper – must be prepared with glue size and/or primer to prevent them absorbing the oil in the paint; if too much oil is absorbed, the paint may eventually crack.

Canvas

The most popular surface is canvas, which has a unique responsiveness and plenty of tooth to hold the paint. It is available in various weights and in fine, medium and coarse-grained textures. You can buy it either glued onto stiff board, ready-stretched and primed on a wooden stretcher frame, or by the metre from a roll.

Canvas weight is measured in ounces per square yard. The higher the number, the greater the density of threads and the better the quality. The two main types are linen and cotton.

Linen is the best canvas. It has a fine, even grain that is free of knots and easy to paint on. It is expensive but very durable.

Cotton Good-quality cotton canvas, such as cotton duck, comes in various grades. It stretches well and is the best alternative to linen – at about half the price. Lighter-weight canvases are recommended for practice work only.

Boards and papers

Prepared canvas boards are inexpensive and are ideal for practice work.

Hardboard is an excellent yet inexpensive support for oils. Plywood, chipboard and MDF (medium-density fibreboard) are also suitable, and can be prepared with primer if you like a white surface, or simply apply a coat of glue size or PVA for a neutral mid-toned surface.

Oil sketching paper is prepared for oil painting and is textured to resemble canvas weave. Sold in pads it is handy for outdoor sketches and practice work.

Use a mahl stick to steady your hand when painting details and fine lines. Place the padded end on a dry section of the painting or on the edge of the canvas. Then rest your painting arm on the stick.

PAINTING ACCESSORIES

Painting in oils can be messy, so the most essential accessories are large jars or tins to hold solvents for cleaning brushes, and a supply of cotton rags and newspaper! The following items are not essential, but useful.

Painting knives have flexible blades and cranked handles, and can be used instead of a brush to apply thick paint.

Palette knives have a long, straight, flexible blade with a rounded tip. They are used for cleaning the palette and mixing paint.

Dippers are small, open cups that clip onto the edge of your palette to hold mediums and thinners during painting.

Mahl stick This is used to steady your hand when painting small details or fine lines. It consists of a long handle made of wood or metal, with a cushion at one end.

BASIC TECHNIQUES

PRIMING THE SUPPORT

Canvas, board and other supports for oil painting must be sealed before being used, otherwise oils from the paint layer seep down into the canvas, leaving the paint impoverished and eventually prone to flaking or cracking. The traditional method is to apply a "ground" consisting of a layer of glue size and one or more layers of emulsion or gesso primer. The modern alternative is acrylic primer, which can be applied directly to the support without the need for glue size and is ready to paint on in about 30 minutes.

An economical primer that can be used on board (but not on stretched canvas) is ordinary matt white household paint, which provides a sympathetic semi-absorbent ground. However, use only good-quality paint, because cheap emulsions will quickly yellow.

Smooth surfaces such as hardboard (masonite) should first be lightly sanded to provide a key for the primer. Using a household paintbrush, apply two or three thin coats, each one at a right angle to the one before.

Allow each coat to dry before the next is applied. If you prefer to work on a more textured painting surface, apply the primer using rough brushstrokes, or mix it with equal proportions of acrylic texture paste, which is available from art supply stores.

TONED GROUNDS

A pure white canvas can be inhibiting to work on, especially for beginners, and it is difficult to assess colours and tones against white. Most artists prefer to tone the ground with a thin layer of paint, diluted with white (mineral) spirit (see page 17). Subdued earths, ochres and blue-greys are normally chosen for toning because they provide a neutral mid-tone from which you can work out towards the darks and lights. If some of the

Priming Supports

1
Using a decorating brush, apply a smooth coat of primer and leave to dry.

2
Apply the second coat at right angles to the first to give a smooth, even surface.

Toned Grounds

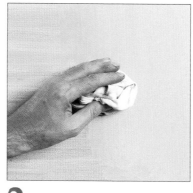

1

Dilute the paint with turpentine or white spirit to a thin consistency and scrub it on vigorously with a large flat brush or a decorating brush.

2

If you prefer a smooth ground, work over the wet paint with a soft rag to even out the brushstrokes. The toned ground must be completely dry before you start to paint on it. With oils this can take up to **24 hours**.

ground is left exposed it will give an overall sense of unity to the painting.

PALETTE LAYOUT

It is said that if your palette is messy, your painting will be messy, so it is a good idea to get into the habit of laying out your colours in the same systematic

The colours on this palette are arranged in the order of the spectrum. Clockwise from the bottom, they are: cadmium red, alizarin crimson, burnt sienna, yellow ochre, cadmium yellow, lemon yellow, viridian, cobalt blue, French ultramarine and cobalt violet, with white in the centre.

A wet oily surface can be difficult to work over. Use a piece of absorbent paper to blot off the excess paint, leaving a surface with more "grip".

order each time you paint. That way, you will automatically know where each colour is without having to search for it, and you will be able to concentrate on observing your subject. There are several systems for laying out colours. Some painters prefer to arrange their colours along one side of the palette in the order of the spectrum, with white and the earth colours on the other side; others use a light to dark or warm to cool sequence. Whatever system you choose, it's a good idea to put a large squeeze of white paint (used in most mixes) in the centre so the other colours can be easily combined with it.

HOLDING THE PALETTE

The traditional kidney-shaped palette has a bevelled thumbhole for maximum comfort when painting at the easel. The curved indent at the leading edge allows you to grasp several brushes and your painting rag in one hand, while painting with the other. Hold the palette in your left hand (if you are right-handed), resting it on your forearm and fitting it up against your body.

MAKING CORRECTIONS

One of the advantages of painting in oils is that corrections can be made easily while the paint is still wet, or simply painted over when the paint is dry. An unsatisfactory passage can be removed while the paint is still fresh by scraping off the unwanted paint with a palette knife. This will leave a ghost of the original image and will form a helpful base on which to begin again. Alternatively, the scraped area can be completely removed with a rag soaked in turpentine.

If the canvas becomes clogged with thick paint and too slippery to work over, you can remove surface paint with absorbent paper, such as newspaper or tissue. Press the paper over the wet canvas and gently smooth it down with the flat of your hand, then carefully peel the paper away. The paper absorbs the excess oily paint,

At first when you try to hold your palette and everything else you may find it uncomfortable, but very soon it will become second nature.

leaving a cleaner surface on which to work. This process is called "tonking", after Henry Tonks, a former professor of painting at the Slade School of Art in London.

BRUSH CARE

Take good care of your paint-brushes and they will give you many years of service. You should clean your brushes at the end of every painting day, and never leave them soaking in solvent with the bristles touching the bottom of the container.

After rinsing the brush in white spirit and thoroughly wiping with a rag, soap the bristles well with plenty of pure household soap (not detergent) and warm water. Then rub the brush around gently in your palm, rinsing now and then. Continue rubbing and rinsing until all the paint is removed. Rinse finally in warm water, shake dry, then smooth the bristles into shape. Leave the brush to dry, bristle end up, in a jar.

It is essential to remove every trace of paint, especially near the ferule. Repeat the soaping until no trace of pigment appears in the lather.

Squaring Up

You may wish to base an oil painting on a sketch or a photographic image; but it is often difficult to maintain the accuracy of the drawing when enlarging or reducing a reference source to the size of your canvas or board. A simple method of transferring an image in a different scale is by squaring up (sometimes called scaling up).

Using a pencil and ruler, draw a grid of equal-sized squares over the sketch or photograph. The more complex the image, the more squares you should draw. If you wish to avoid marking the original, make a photocopy of it and draw the grid onto this. Alternatively, draw the grid onto a sheet of clear acetate placed over the original, using a felt-tip pen.

Then construct an enlarged version of the grid on your support, using light charcoal lines. This grid must have the same number of squares as the smaller one. The size of the squares will depend on the degree of enlargement required: for example, if you are doubling the size of your reference material, make the squares twice the size of the squares on the original reference drawing or photograph.

When the grid is complete, transfer the image that appears in each square of the original to its equivalent square on the support. The larger squares on the working sheet serve to enlarge the original image. You are, in effect, breaking down a large-scale problem into smaller, more manageable areas.

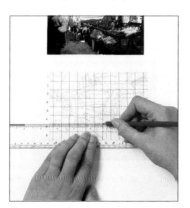

1
Make a sketch from the reference photograph and draw a grid of squares over it.

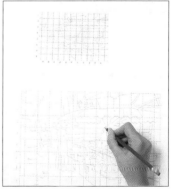

2
Draw a grid of larger squares onto the support and transfer the detail from the sketch, square by square.

GALLERY

O il paint is a highly versatile and responsive medium, capable of producing an infinite range of textures and effects. Used straight from the tube it produces thick, rich impastos in which the quality of the paint surface and the mark of the brush become an integral part of the finished image. Thinly diluted it can be used to apply delicate, translucent glazes that seem to glow with an inner light. And there are many fascinating variations between these two extremes.

On the following pages you will find a selection of oil paintings by contemporary artists, revealing a diversity of technique and breadth of imagination which, it is hoped, will inspire you to try out new techniques or to tackle unfamiliar subjects.

Autumn Window
Timothy Easton
61 x 51cm (24 x 20in)

Easton has exploited the richness and lustre of oil paints in conveying the warm glow of autumn sunshine on this scene. The wonderful vibrancy of the picture stems, too, from the use of complementary colours – the predominantly warm, yellowish hues are offset by touches of cool violet.

Tulips in the Sun
Trevor Chamberlain
15 x 21cm (6 x 8in)

You don't have to venture far
afield to find interesting subjects
to paint. To an artist with an
inquiring eye, just about anything
will make a good picture – much
depends on how you crop the
subject and compose the image.
Here, the artist was taken with the
loose informality of a clump of
tulips growing in his garden.

Washing on the Line
James Horton
30 x 41cm (12 x 16in)

Here we have another seemingly
mundane subject – a line of
washing – which has been
transformed into an appealing
image through the artist's astute
handling of colour and
composition. With a moving
subject such as this you have to
work fast to capture the essence,
relying heavily on your visual
memory.

Above Beck Hole, near Whitby
David Curtis
56 x 46cm (22 x 18in)

The high viewpoint here affords an opportunity to convey a thrilling impression of space, light and atmosphere. The painting was executed over two consecutive days, the artist returning at the same time each day when the light conditions were consistent. The finished piece captures the feel of a blisteringly hot day, with the distant landscape enveloped in a bluish heat haze.

Orange Sunshade
Barry Freeman
25 x 36cm (10 x 14in)

The beach is a rich source of imagery for the artist, so make sure you pack your sketchbook along with your suntan cream! Intrigued by the refreshingly simple arrangement of shapes and colours in this little group, Freeman painted it exactly as he saw it, apart from moving the beach ball from the right to the left in order to improve the compositional balance of the image.

Apollo
Olwen Tarrant
61 x 91cm (24 x 36in)

Tarrant's paintings are carefully designed with an eye to colour, shape and overall pattern. The flat, matt quality of the paint surface and the use of broad blocks of colour accentuate the formal abstract qualities of the image, though it also reads as a collection of recognizable objects. There are many subtle echoes and repetitions that activate the shallow space, leading the eye around the painting and giving it a satisfying harmony.

Bathers on the Strand
John Denahy
18 x 27cm (7 x 10½in)

For Denahy the marks and textures of the paint are in themselves an exciting and enjoyable part of the painting process. He mixes his colours with a little white spirit or alkyd medium to a stiff, matt, "chalky" consistency and applies them with brushes, knives and scrapers. Rich and complex interactions of colour are achieved by loosely dragging and scumbling over thinly glazed underlayers.

Full Summer
Peter Graham
36 x 25cm (14 x 10in)

This painting was executed rapidly on site in order to capture the mood of the moment. Beneath the apparent careless vivacity of surface, however, lies a carefully thought-out structure; the verticals of the trees are counterpointed by the sweeping curves of paint in the foreground, which lead the eye to groups of figures. These, in turn, are positioned to lead the eye through the picture in a rhythmic way, the tiny dots of red on the clothing acting as visual "stepping stones".

Dusk, San Mario
James Horton
13 x 23cm (5 x 9in)

Painted with dash and bravura, this tiny study effectively conveys the atmosphere of a wet and windy evening in St Mark's Square, Venice. Horton was less interested in recording the physical features of the scene, more with capturing the eerie quality of the light. It was essential to gauge the tonal values accurately, and working on a mid-toned ground enabled him to work out to the lights and darks more easily.

PAINTING "ALLA PRIMA"

This delightful and exuberant landscape was painted on-the-spot in the hills of Tuscany in southern Italy. In order to capture the movement of the scudding clouds and the rapidly changing light, the painting had to be executed quickly, in one sitting – a method known as "alla prima".

The artist started by blocking in the broad areas of the composition with thinned paint, which is easy to manipulate when working fast. He continued building up the colour, applying it in wide sweeps and rapid scumbles that give energy and movement to the scene.

When painting "alla prima" you have to be constantly aware of how the different elements of the image – line, mass, tone and colour – interact. To achieve balance and unity, the artist worked on all areas of the composition at once, rather than painting one area in detail before starting on the next; he kept his brush moving around the canvas, working from sky to land and back again, bringing all areas of the image to a similar level of detail at each stage.

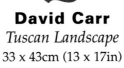

David Carr
Tuscan Landscape
33 x 43cm (13 x 17in)

ALLA PRIMA TECHNIQUE

Alla prima is an Italian expression meaning "at the first", and describes a technique in which a painting is completed in one session, instead of being built up layer by layer. The French Impressionists and their forerunners – Constable (1776–1837) and Corot (1796–1875) – were great exponents of this method, which is particularly well suited to painting outdoors.

In *alla prima* painting there is generally little or no initial underpainting, although artists sometimes make a rapid underdrawing in charcoal or thinned paint to act as a guide. Each patch of colour is then laid down more or less as it will appear in the finished painting, or worked wet-into-wet with adjacent colours. The idea with this kind of painting is to capture the essence of the subject in an intuitive way, using vigorous, expressive brush-strokes and minimal colour mixing.

One of the great advantages of *alla prima* painting is that it creates an extremely stable paint surface. Whereas a painting that is composed of several built up layers may be prone to cracking eventually, due to the uneven drying rates of the different layers, a painting completed in one session dries uniformly, even when it is laid on thickly.

The ability to apply paint quickly and confidently is the key to the *alla prima* approach. It is, of course, always possible to scrape away and rework unsuccessful areas of a painting, but in doing so there is a danger that some of the freshness and spontaneity will be lost. It is therefore very important to start with a clear idea in your mind of what you want to convey in your painting, working with a limited palette can sometimes be a good idea, as you will not be tempted to include any unnecessary detail.

TUSCAN LANDSCAPE

Materials and Equipment

• SHEET OF PRIMED CANVAS OR BOARD • OIL COLOURS: CADMIUM RED, CADMIUM YELLOW, CADMIUM LEMON, YELLOW OCHRE, COBALT GREEN, VIRIDIAN, FRENCH ULTRAMARINE, COBALT BLUE, CERULEAN, RAW UMBER, BURNT SIENNA AND TITANIUM WHITE • BRISTLE BRUSHES: LARGE AND SMALL ROUNDS, AND MEDIUM FILBERT • SMALL LETTERING BRUSH OR ROUND SOFT-HAIR BRUSH • TURPENTINE • LINSEED OIL • RAG AND WHITE SPIRIT FOR CLEANING

1

First establish the position of the horizon line, then work straight into the sky area. To create a warm base colour for the clouds, mix a soft yellow from yellow ochre and titanium white; for the patch of blue sky, use ultramarine and white. Dilute the paint thinly with a 50–50 mix of turpentine and linseed oil and apply it rapidly with broad, sweeping strokes, using the belly – not the tip – of a large round-bristle brush.

2

To enhance the mellow warmth of the Italian landscape, the greens and yellows of the hills and fields are underpainted in their complementary colours – reds and blues, respectively. Using a medium filbert brush, paint the most distant hills with a thin wash of pale pink mixed from cadmium red, white and a touch of cadmium yellow. Strengthen the mix with more red and less white for the nearer hills. Underpaint the wheat fields with cobalt blue, then map in the dark trees and hedges with a mix of burnt sienna and cadmium red.

3

With a thin mix of ultramarine and white, block in the patches of blue sky and roughly outline the masses of cumulus cloud. Again, use the flattened belly of the bristle head to make broad, energetic strokes, letting the brush marks convey a sense of movement.

4

Now work on the distant sky and hills to create a sense of the land and sky disappearing over the horizon. Mix a cool, soft green from cobalt green and white. Drag this over the furthest hills, letting the pink undercolour show through the green. Then mix a soft pinkish yellow from cadmium yellow, white and a touch of cadmium red and paint a narrow band of this right along the horizon line, just above the hills, to create the effect of misty light in the distance.

With a small round brush, mix a dark green from viridian and yellow ochre and define the trees and hedgerows between the fields, dragging the paint on with the side of the brush.

5

Mix ultramarine and white, then add touches of burnt sienna and yellow ochre until you have a warm grey. Paint the shadow sides of the clouds with a large round brush, scrubbing the paint on with vigorous brushmarks that give a sense of movement. Always remember to keep your cloud shadows consistent with the direction of the light – here the sun is at the top right, so the cloud shadows are on the left of the cloud masses.

6

Paint the patchwork of wheatfields using a medium filbert brush and varied mixtures of cadmium yellow and yellow ochre, plus cadmium lemon for the brightly lit fields. With a large round brush, paint the lit areas of cloud by working into the grey clouds with a warm, creamy white mixed from white, cadmium yellow, cadmium red and yellow ochre. Use slightly thicker paint and scrubby, scumbled strokes to create the effect of towering heaps of cloud, particularly in the foreground. As the clouds recede into the distance, use flatter strokes.

7

Neutralize the yellow mixes with some grey mixed earlier and, with a medium filbert brush, darken areas where the clouds cast shadows onto the land. Add definition to fields and hedgerows using paint that is fluid, but with body. (Here a sable lettering brush, which is round but with a flat point and long bristles is used to give smooth, fluid lines. If you don't have one, a small round soft-hair brush will do.) For the hedgerows, use a dark mix of viridian, ultramarine and raw umber. Bring the nearest fields forward with mixtures of cadmium red, yellow and lemon.

8

The sky appears paler and cooler as it recedes towards the horizon. To recreate this effect, mix three shades of blue on your palette and then blend them together on the canvas with a medium filbert brush so that they merge gently into one another. Start at the top with ultramarine and white, then introduce cerulean and white as you work downwards. Near the horizon, use white with hints of cadmium yellow and red added.

Scumble a mixture of white and a hint of yellow ochre onto the sunlit tops of the clouds with rough, scrubby marks.

9

Finally, tie the painting together by echoing some of the sky colours in the land below, adding touches of ultramarine and white, and yellow ochre and white to the fields. Strengthen the shadows on the fields with dark greens. Try not to overwork the painting – keep it fresh and lively. If the paint becomes too opaque and dense, you can scratch into it with the end of a paintbrush to reclaim the colour of the underpainting, as shown here.

Technique
2

IMPASTO

Impasto painting exploits to the full the rich, buttery consistency of oil paint. Because thickly impasted paint retains the strokes made with the brush or knife, the marks produced are an expressive element in the finished work and help to produce a pleasing, tactile surface.

The impasto technique is often used in direct, "alla prima" painting, as the thick paint and rapid brushstrokes allow the picture to be completed quickly and spontaneously. To capture an impression of intense heat and sunlight on this Italian landscape the artist worked quickly and freely, blocking in the broad forms and areas of colour with thin paint before starting to build up the overall image with thick, rich impastos. With this thicker paint, the marks of the brush can be used to describe and follow form as well as to indicate the texture of particular areas. Compare, for example, the slurred strokes of creamy paint used for the distant fields with the heavier, stippled marks used to suggest the foliage in the foreground. The thicker strokes in the foreground bring that area forward in the picture plane, pushing back the distant landscape and increasing the sense of recession.

Derek Daniells
Monastery, Tuscany
46 x 36cm (18 x 14in)

THE IMPASTO TECHNIQUE

When oil paint is applied thickly and liberally so that it protrudes from the surface of the support and retains the marks and ridges left by the brush, it is called impasto.

Some pictures are painted entirely in impasto, the thick paint and descriptive brushwork creating a lively, energetic surface. In others, impasto is reserved for certain areas such as details and high-lights, or it is used to accentuate the focal point of the picture. Vincent van Gogh exploited the expressive potential of impasto in his paintings, often squeezing the paint straight from the tube and "sculpting" it into generous sweeps and swirls. In contrast, Rembrandt mainly used thin paint and reserved small but telling strokes of thick, light-reflecting paint to show the highlights on skin tones, jewellery and clothing in his portraits.

Paint for impasto work can be applied with a brush or a painting knife. The paint should be of a buttery consistency and may be used straight from the tube or diluted with a small amount of turpentine or medium so that it is malleable, yet thick enough to stand proud of the support.

Using heavy applications of oil paint in this way can be expensive, but fortu-nately thickening mediums specially for use with impasto work are avail-able; they bulk out the paint without increasing the drying time.

Bristle brushes are best for impasto work because they hold a lot of paint. Load the brush with plenty of colour and dab it generously onto the canvas, teasing it into peaks and ridges or spreading it out in luscious bands that reflect a lot of light.

MONASTERY, TUSCANY

1

Prepare your canvas 24 hours in advance by tinting it with a wash of yellow ochre thinly diluted with turpentine. Apply the paint with a large flat brush, then rub with a soft cloth to eliminate the brushstrokes and leave a smooth surface. When the canvas is dry, use a small round soft-hair brush to sketch in the main outlines of the composition with a thin mix of burnt sienna. (If you feel hesitant about drawing with paint, use charcoal instead.)

Materials and Equipment

- SHEET OF PRIMED CANVAS OR BOARD • OIL COLOURS: CADMIUM RED, CADMIUM YELLOW, YELLOW OCHRE, LEMON YELLOW, NAPLES YELLOW, CERULEAN, PRUSSIAN BLUE, COBALT BLUE, COBALT VIOLET, BURNT SIENNA AND TITANIUM WHITE • SMALL ROUND SOFT-HAIR BRUSH
- LARGE, MEDIUM AND SMALL FLAT BRISTLE BRUSHES
- PAINTING KNIFE • SOFT CLOTH
- DISTILLED TURPENTINE
- PURIFIED LINSEED OIL
- ALKYD MEDIUM

2

Block in the terracotta roofs of the monastery with a thinly diluted mix of cadmium red and cadmium yellow, applied with a medium-sized flat bristle brush. Mix a cool brown for the walls in shadow using yellow ochre, cobalt violet and a touch of cobalt blue. Using slightly thicker paint now, mix a pale blue from cobalt blue and titanium white and block in the sky and distant fields with roughly scumbled strokes applied with a painting knife.

3

Mix a pale, cool green from cerulean, lemon yellow and white. Apply bands of this colour across the background with a medium-sized flat bristle brush to indicate the green fields and trees in the distance. Make the bands narrower and closer together the nearer they are to the horizon, to suggest perspective and distance.

4

Add further bands of colour in the distance, this time using a mix of cobalt blue, cobalt violet and white to suggest the hazy, bluish light on the far horizon. Soften and "knock back" the distant landscape by lightly feathering over the wet colours with a dry brush. Mix a thin wash of Prussian blue and rough in the darks in the foreground trees and foliage. Use a fairly dry brush and scumble the paint on lightly so that it dries quickly.

5

Continue blocking in the broad areas of light and shadow in the foreground foliage. Mix cerulean, lemon yellow and white for the warm, sunlit greens and Prussian blue and white for the cool, bluish tints. Use similar colours to indicate the cobbled road. The paint at this block-in stage is still quite thin and "dry"; this will allow you to build up a rich impasto on top in the later stages without creating an unpleasant, churned-up surface.

6

Mix cadmium red, cadmium yellow and a hint of burnt sienna and block in the shadowed parts of the roofs. Work into the outline of the tree on the left with loose, broken strokes using a small flat brush to give the effect of rooftops glimpsed through the foliage.

Mix Naples yellow and a tiny touch of cadmium red and block in the sunlit walls of the monastery. Mix a warm grey from yellow ochre and cobalt violet and indicate the windows, painting each one with a single stroke of the small flat brush.

7

Begin to build up a thicker impasto now. Work over the roofs with the same colours used in the thin underlayers, this time mixing the paint with a little medium to give it a buttery consistency that emphasizes the impasto. Lay on the colours with a well-loaded medium-sized flat brush, letting the marks of the brush show so that they add texture and interest to the paint surface.

8

Add more detail to the distant landscape, using a small flat brush to apply small, broken touches of thick colour that suggest the shimmering haze around the fields, houses and trees under the hot Mediterranean sun. Mix cerulean and white for the sky, then add touches of cobalt blue and cobalt violet and work over the lines of the trees with lightly scumbled strokes. Paint the corn fields with varied tones mixed from yellow ochre, Naples yellow, cadmium yellow and white. Suggest the rooftops glimpsed between the trees with cadmium red, cadmium yellow and white.

9

Returning to the foreground, continue to build up texture and define the individual clumps of foliage with small strokes and dabs of thick paint worked in different directions. Emphasize the dark, shadowy tones by adding touches of cobalt blue and cobalt violet to the greens. For the sunlit foliage mix lemon yellow and white.

10

Now work on the cobbled road, again using short strokes and dabs of colour but laying them on horizontally. To show dappled sunlight, use mixes of Prussian blue, cobalt blue and cadmium red, with a little white for the shadows cast by the hanging foliage. For the sunlit areas, use varied tones of cadmium red, yellow ochre and white.

If you find it difficult to apply fresh paint over wet paint without muddying the colours, allow the painting to dry off for a day or two. Continue building tones in the foliage with small strokes of broken colour, adding more detail and depth.

Technique

3

USING A TONED GROUND

There are times when it is appropriate to paint directly onto a white canvas, but most oil painters prefer to tint the ground with a colour that sets a key for the painting. In this interior scene small patches of the umber ground remain exposed throughout the picture, their neutral colour helping to unify the composition and enhancing the impression of soft, cool light penetrating the room from the window behind.

It is important that the toned ground is completely dry before you paint over it. An oil ground usually takes around 24 hours to dry thoroughly, but you can save time by using acrylic paint instead. This dries in minutes, allowing you to overpaint in oils straight away. The other great advantage is that acrylic paint acts as both a sealing agent and a primer, so you don't need to size and prime the support as you would for oils. (Never apply acrylics on a ground that has been sized and primed for oils, however, as this may lead to eventual cracking of the paint film.)

James Horton
French Interior
25 x 18cm (10 x 7in)

TONING THE GROUND

A primed white ground can be rather intimidating to begin painting on and can also give you a false "reading" of the colours and tones you apply, especially in the early stages when you've no other colours to relate them to. The way to avoid this problem is by toning the ground with a wash of neutral colour prior to painting.

A toned ground provides a more sympathetic surface to work on, acting as a unifying mid-tone against which you can judge your lights and darks more accurately. Generally it is best to choose a subtle, muted colour somewhere between the lightest and the darkest colours in the painting. Diluted earth colours such as Venetian red, raw sienna or burnt umber work very well,

as do soft greys and greens. Some artists prefer to begin with a ground that will harmonize with the dominant colour of the subject; for instance, a soft pink or yellow ground for an evening sky. Others prefer a ground that provides a quiet contrast, such as a warm red-brown that will enhance the greens used in a landscape.

To tone the ground, dilute the paint to a thin, "orange juice" consistency with turpentine or white (mineral) spirit and apply it freely and vigorously over the white priming with a household decorating brush or a rag soaked in turpentine. If you prefer a smooth, more regular effect, work over the wet paint with a damp, lint-free rag to even out the brushmarks.

FRENCH INTERIOR

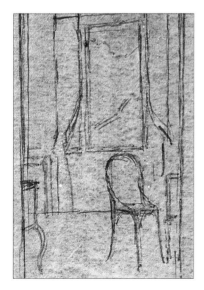

1

Prepare the toned ground about 24 hours in advance – it must be thoroughly dry before starting to paint. Mix raw umber with a little French ultramarine and dilute it to a thin consistency with turpentine. Apply this all over the board using a 25mm (1in) decorating brush.

Sketch in the main outlines of the composition using thinly diluted French ultramarine and a small sable brush.

Materials and Equipment

• SHEET OF PRIMED HARDBOARD OR MDF • OIL COLOURS: CADMIUM RED, ALIZARIN CRIMSON, VERMILION, CADMIUM ORANGE, CADMIUM YELLOW, YELLOW OCHRE, LEMON YELLOW, TERRE VERTE, FRENCH ULTRAMARINE, COBALT BLUE, RAW UMBER, BURNT SIENNA, TITANIUM WHITE AND IVORY BLACK • 25MM (1IN) DECORATING BRUSH • OIL-PAINTING BRUSHES: SMALL SABLE OR SYNTHETIC, MEDIUM-SIZED ROUND BRISTLE, SMALL ROUND BRISTLE, SABLE OR SYNTHETIC RIGGER • PURE LINSEED OIL • DAMMAR VARNISH • DISTILLED TURPENTINE

2

From this point, mix your colours with a medium consisting of linseed oil, dammar varnish and turpentine. Using a medium size round bristle brush, rough in the walls around the open doorway with a warm brown mixed from burnt sienna, raw umber and titanium white. Vary the proportions of these colours and add touches of lemon yellow and terre verte to create subtle shifts in tone and temperature. Don't apply the paint in a flat wash but scuff it on with broken strokes, letting the ground colour show through.

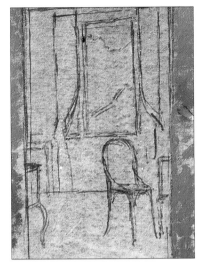

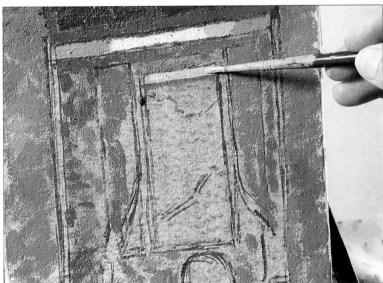

3

Use the same colour and the same technique to paint the curtains at the window. Start to block in the wall around the window using loose strokes of ultramarine greyed with a little yellow ochre, interspersed with strokes of greenish grey mixed from raw umber and yellow ochre. Use a smaller round brush to paint the bright reflection on the ceiling with white and a mix of cobalt blue, alizarin crimson and white. For the pink strip at the top of the window, mix vermilion and white.

4

Now paint the view glimpsed through the window. Mix white and a tiny drop of alizarin crimson for the sky, then suggest the trees with varied mixtures of lemon yellow, terre verte, cobalt blue and white. Use a greater proportion of blue and green for the darker tones and more yellow and white for the lighter tones. Paint the window frame with raw umber and the sill with cobalt blue, alizarin crimson and white.

5

Add more colour to the curtains with strokes of raw umber and white. Loosely paint the chair back with a mix of French ultramarine, yellow ochre and a little ivory black. Then suggest the reflective surface of the floor using mainly white, broken with a little burnt sienna and alizarin crimson. Apply the colour in loose patches, letting the ground colour form the mid-tone.

6

Paint the pieces of furniture glimpsed through the doorway, using black, cadmium red and alizarin crimson for the dark wood and burnt sienna and raw umber for the lighter wood of the chair legs. For the chair seat, mix white, ultramarine and alizarin. Use the same mixture used on the back, lightened with more white, for the shadow on the chair seat.

7

Lighten the tone of the wall beneath the window with a warm grey mixed from ultramarine, yellow ochre, white and a hint of black, loosely applied over the underlayer of brown. Block in the base of the shutters with vermilion and white, then add warm highlights on the curtains where the light shines through the fabric, using a small round brush and mixtures of cadmium orange, cadmium yellow and white.

8

Now that the close tones of the interior are established, you can adjust the brighter tones of the sunlit view outside to the correct pitch. Here the greens of the hills and trees need to be lighter and cooler to push them back in space. Mix cobalt, alizarin and white for the distant hills, then block in the medium-toned foliage with varied mixtures of white, lemon yellow, terre verte and a hint of cobalt blue. Use a rigger brush, which has long, flexible hairs, to define the edge of the window frame with a very thin line of black.

9

Finally, mix a sludgy grey from raw umber, ultramarine, burnt sienna and yellow ochre and use this to paint the shadows cast by the furniture legs on the shiny floor. Use the rigger brush again, applying the paint with slightly wavering strokes.

WORKING "FAT OVER LEAN"

Painting "from lean to fat" is the time-honoured method of building up an oil painting in layers, especially when mixing the paint with turpentine and linseed oil. Put simply, this means using thin, "lean" paint in the early stages and gradually increasing the oil content in the upper layers. Along with sound preparation of the canvas or board, this method can prevent one of the problems associated with oil painting – the possible cracking of the paint surface.

For this still-life painting the artist started out with very thin paint diluted to an "orange juice" consistency with turpentine. This allows the white primer to shine through and give luminosity to the succeeding colours. Because the paint was so lean it dried quickly, allowing further layers to be applied almost immediately. The artist then continued working with layers of increasingly thick paint, building up depth and luminosity in the colours.

Peter Graham
Bouquet and Fruit
63½ x 56cm (25 x 22in)

WORKING "FAT OVER LEAN"

"Fat" describes paint that comes straight from the tube or is mixed with an oily medium. "Lean" describes paint that has been thinned with turpentine or white (mineral) spirit. The golden rule in oil painting, particularly when building up a painting in layers, is always to paint fat over lean. If lean paint is applied over fat, you could find that your painting begins to crack eventually – something that may take weeks, months or even years to become apparent.

The reason for this has to do with the way oil paints dry. The oils in the paint do not evaporate; they oxidize and harden on exposure to the air. This process can often take several months, and during this time the paint surface first expands, then shrinks a little. Fat paint is more flexible than lean paint, and takes longer to dry. It follows, then, that if lean paint is applied over fat, the top layer will dry before the lower, more oily one, has

finished shrinking. The movement in the lower layers may cause the hardened lean paint on top to crack and even flake off.

Thus, when painting in layers, you should begin with an underpainting that is thinner and faster-drying than subsequent layers. For example, start with paint thinned with turpentine or a fast-drying alkyd medium. The next layer may consist of either undiluted tube paint, or paint mixed with turpentine and a little oil. Any successive layers may contain either the same or increasing amounts of oil, but they should not contain less oil.

Generally speaking, the *alla prima* method – completing the painting in one session with a single layer of opaque paint – presents fewer problems. When paint is worked wet-into-wet, the danger of cracking is considerably less because the paint films dry together rather than at different rates.

Preliminary underpainting in thin, lean paint provides a basis for the application of subsequent layers of oilier paint.

BOUQUET AND FRUIT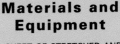

Left: In this still-life arrangement, gaily coloured cloths and scraps of fabric are carefully arranged to break up the picture space in an interesting way. The white flowers and objects act as a foil for the brighter hues.

Materials and Equipment

- SHEET OF STRETCHED AND PRIMED CANVAS • OIL COLOURS: ROSE MADDER DEEP, CADMIUM SCARLET, CADMIUM RED, PERMANENT MAGENTA, MAUVE, ALIZARIN CRIMSON, CADMIUM LEMON, CADMIUM YELLOW, NAPLES YELLOW LIGHT, COBALT TURQUOISE, EMERALD GREEN, PRUSSIAN GREEN, COBALT GREEN, VIRIDIAN, FRENCH ULTRAMARINE, COBALT BLUE, INDIGO, RAW SIENNA, RAW UMBER AND TITANIUM WHITE
- BRISTLE BRUSHES: LARGE FLAT, MEDIUM LONG FLAT, SMALL LONG FLAT AND FAN BLENDER
- SMALL ROUND SYNTHETIC-HAIR BRUSH • COTTON RAG • PALETTE KNIFE • DISTILLED TURPENTINE
- PURIFIED LINSEED OIL

1

Position the main elements of the composition with loose, vigorous strokes, using paint thinly diluted with turpentine and applied with a large flat bristle brush. Use French ultramarine and indigo for the blue backcloth and cobalt turquoise for the small bowl on the left. Block in the limes and apples on either side of the white vase with emerald green, cobalt green and Prussian green and use the same colours for the flower foliage. Block in the vase itself with titanium white mixed with a little cadmium lemon, adding a hint of mauve on the shadow side.

2

Continue painting loosely, developing all areas at the same time. Define the shape of the white daisies "negatively", by painting the blue backcloth behind them. Paint the scraps of red fabric using permanent magenta on the left and cadmium red on the right. Mix cadmium yellow, white and raw sienna for the pieces of yellow fabric. Use raw umber to strengthen outlines and block in shadows, and lift out highlights by rubbing back to the white canvas with a rag. As the paint is thin there will be spatters and runs, but they will be covered up later.

3

With the broad masses of the composition mapped in you can now start to refine and define. Add a little linseed oil to the turpentine in your jar or dipper to thicken and enrich the paint, and go over the shadows on the white vase with soft greys mixed from varied proportions of white, mauve and a little cobalt green. Use the same mixes to paint the shadows on the fruit dish, helping to define its shape.

4

Mix a bright orange from cadmium scarlet and cadmium lemon and suggest the floral pattern on the fruit dish. Switch to a medium-sized long flat brush for this, using the body of the brush to paint each petal with a single stroke.

5

Slightly increase the proportion of linseed oil in your painting medium and begin to model the rounded forms of the apples on the right with light, medium and dark tones of green. First block in the mid-tone with viridian, cadmium yellow and a hint of raw sienna. Then put in the darker shadow tones with Prussian green. For the lighter tops of the apples use a mix of emerald green and Naples yellow light, with touches of cadmium lemon for the highlights. Twist and turn the brush as you work, following the forms of the apples with your brushstrokes.

6

Paint the fruit in the bowl. Mix varied amounts of white, emerald green, Naples yellow light and cadmium lemon for the apple and pear, both of which are lighter in colour than the apples farther back. Mix cadmium yellow, Naples yellow light and white for the apricot, and block in the plum at the back with a near-black mixed from rose madder deep and Prussian green.

Block in the shadows cast by the apples on the white cloth with mixes of white, mauve and cobalt green applied with overlaid strokes. Use the edge of a palette knife to scrape out the highlights on the blue backcloth.

7

Work on the green bowl with softly blended strokes of cobalt turquoise and cobalt green lightened with white. Combine white with hints of viridian and cadmium lemon and use to suggest the shiny highlights. Then use a medium-sized long flat brush to paint the blue-green cloth with varied mixes of cobalt turquoise, French ultramarine, white and indigo.

8

Model the forms of the limes using the same mixtures used for the apples but with a greater proportion of emerald green to make the limes slightly more acid in colour. Mix rose madder deep and Prussian green for the plum behind the limes. Use the same colour to define the folds in the red cloth. Paint the stripes on the green bowl with cobalt blue, using a small flat brush. Put in the brightest highlights with small, thick strokes of pure white. Then use a fan blender, with very light pressure, to soften and blend the tones on the inside of the bowl.

9

Now work on the bouquet of daisies. With a medium-sized long flat brush, define the forms of the leaves, using Prussian green for the darkest areas and various mixes of cobalt green, Naples yellow light and viridian for the mid- to light tones. Switch to a small long flat brush and start to define some of the daisy petals. Use pure white for those at the front, and white "dirtied" with hints of raw sienna and cobalt blue for those in shadow near the back. Mix Naples yellow light and cadmium red for the eyes of the daisies.

10

Continue describing the forms of the daisies by painting the shadowy petals with warm and cool greys mixed from varying amounts of raw sienna, cobalt blue, mauve and white. Paint each petal with a single mark, using the long edge of the brush to "imprint" the paint onto the canvas. Here the artist is employing the technique to paint the daisies at the front "negatively", using indigo mixed with alizarin crimson to create sharp definition between the white petals and the dark blue background.

11

Stand back and assess the painting overall, looking for the way tones, colours and shapes relate to each other and making adjustments accordingly. Complete the daisies, adding touches of Naples yellow light here and there to warm up the lighter petals. Add the highlights on the plums with white and a touch of the rose madder deep/Prussian green mix. Deepen the tone of the yellow cloths on the left of the picture with cadmium yellow.

12

To complete the picture, use the tip of a small round soft-hair brush to paint the decorative edging on the fruit dish with a near-black mixed from indigo and alizarin crimson.

EXPRESSIVE BRUSHWORK

One of the greatest pleasures of oil painting is the way the paint responds to the brush, and for most artists the actual use of the paint and the resulting marks and textures are in themselves an exciting and enjoyable part of the painting process. In addition, the visible sign of the brush becomes an outward mark of the artist's individuality – a personal calligraphy, as unique as his or her handwriting.

This stormy coastal scene was painted on-the-spot, and the artist's excitement about the subject is reflected in the way he has handled the paint with great freedom and inventiveness. The rapid, expressive brushstrokes, plus the use of both thick and thin paint, convey a marvellous feeling of movement and changing light.

By using paint thinly diluted with a mixture of turpentine and linseed oil the artist was able to work at great speed and with considerable freedom. This approach is particularly useful when working outdoors where the light and weather are liable to change at any moment.

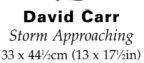

David Carr

Storm Approaching

33 x 44½cm (13 x 17½in)

53

EXPRESSIVE BRUSHWORK

Inexperienced painters often make the mistake of applying the paint with uniform, flat strokes, as if painting a door, but this can render the painting somewhat flat and lifeless.

As you gain more experience, start to think of your painting as a two-dimensional surface in its own right, as well as a recreation of a scene. In other words, think about ways to exploit the expressive possibilities of the paint itself. Not only do different techniques and kinds of brushstrokes help to define forms and suggest the textures of objects, they also give the finished painting a pleasing tactile quality, the character of which is as unique to you as your handwriting.

It is well worth experimenting with a variety of brush shapes – rounds, flats and filberts – as well as bristle brushes and soft-hair brushes, to find out what kind of marks each one can make (see page 14 for more information on brushes). Try making rapid, sweeping strokes and slow, deliberate ones. Hold the brush at various angles to see how this affects the weight of the stroke. Stipple thick paint on with the tip of the brush, or lightly drag it over the surface so that the colour is broken up by the textured weave of the canvas – a technique called drybrush.

Hold the brush where it feels naturally balanced, but not too near the ferule as this limits movement to the fingers and encourages monotonous, restrictive brushmarks. Think of the brush as an extension of yourself. The movement of the arm from the shoulder, through the elbow and wrist, should be fluid, confident and controlled.

STORM APPROACHING

1

Take a deep breath and plunge straight into the painting without making an underdrawing. Mix yellow ochre with a little cadmium red, dilute thinly with turpentine medium, and draw in the low horizon line using the chisel edge of a large filbert brush. Then mass in the main shapes in the sky with thin paint, using varied tones of the yellow ochre/cadmium red mix. Add touches of cerulean and cobalt blue in the upper sky. Work vigorously, using the body of the brush for the broad masses and the edge to make linear marks.

Materials and Equipment

• SHEET OF PRIMED CANVAS OR BOARD • OIL COLOURS: CADMIUM RED, ALIZARIN CRIMSON, YELLOW OCHRE, LEMON YELLOW, CERULEAN, VIRIDIAN, FRENCH ULTRAMARINE, COBALT BLUE, BURNT SIENNA, BURNT UMBER AND TITANIUM WHITE • BRISTLE BRUSHES: LARGE AND MEDIUM-SIZED FILBERTS AND LARGE ROUND • SOFT-HAIR RIGGER BRUSH • PURE LINSEED OIL • DISTILLED TURPENTINE

2

Paint the sea with long horizontal strokes of variegated colour – cerulean, lemon yellow, French ultramarine, and violet mixed from alizarin crimson and ultramarine. Continue blocking in the main shapes, masses and lines in the sky, scrubbing the paint on with lively, vigorous brushstrokes to establish a sense of the towering heaps of storm cloud.

3

Rough in the cliffs on the right with thinly diluted cadmium red, then complete the underpainting of the sky with warm blue-violets mixed from alizarin crimson, ultramarine and lots of titanium white. Here you can see how the artist has worked the brush in various directions, leaving the brushmarks visible so that they contribute a feeling of energy and movement.

4

Make a creamy mixture of viridian and a hint of yellow ochre and white. Switch to a medium-sized filbert brush and use the tip to define the horizon line, the cliffs and the dark patches of sea.

5

Fill in the cliffs with reds, greens and yellows. Modify the colours in the water, lightly stroking pale greys and earths over the wet colours beneath so that they blend and streak. Mix a dark, inky grey from ultramarine, burnt sienna and a little white and paint the dark sweep of storm cloud using a large round brush. Use broad, expansive strokes, but keep the paint fairly thin so that the warm colours in the underpainting show through in places. Leave a narrow sliver of light just above the horizon.

6

Switch to a large filbert brush and paint the patches of blue sky using cerulean, cobalt blue and white. Paint the light cumulus clouds with white warmed with a hint of yellow ochre. Use thicker paint now, applied with plenty of gusto to give the clouds form and movement. Make the clouds smaller and flatter as you near the horizon, to emphasize the illusion of receding space.

7

Streak some of the white cloud mixture across the distant sea, which reflects light from the sky. Now use the large round brush to build up the form of the dark storm cloud with thicker paint, using a cooler grey mixed from ultramarine, burnt umber and a touch of alizarin crimson. Bring some yellow ochre into the clouds at top left, to suggest the sullen light of a stormy day.

8

Mix up some white and add a tiny hint of yellow ochre and cadmium red to warm it. Paint the chalky cliff face with this colour, using a well-loaded soft-hair rigger brush. Use the same brush to work some streaks and wisps into the sky to recreate fragmented clouds being blown by the wind.

9

Mix a dark grey with burnt sienna and ultramarine and paint the dark patches on the water reflected from the clouds above, using the tip of a large round brush. Feather the colour on lightly, letting it pick up some of the wet colours beneath to create streaks of variegated colour.

10

Use the same mixture to emphasize the dramatic sweep of the dark storm clouds with vigorous diagonal strokes. Then switch to the rigger brush again and suggest the waves breaking on the shore with a mixture of white and lemon yellow applied with drybrushed strokes: flick the brush on a rag to remove most of the paint, then drag the brush lightly across the surface to make thin, broken lines.

11

Now use the rigger brush to soften some of the brushstrokes on the light clouds to give them a more fluid, vaporous appearance. Blend some of the cloud edges into the surrounding blue to prevent the clouds appearing "pasted on" to the sky.

12

Add a final dramatic touch to the picture by putting in a long, diagonal sweep of storm cloud that leads the eye from the foreground into the distance. First, mix two colours: yellow ochre, and a grey mixed from yellow ochre, cadmium red and a white. Dip a large round brush, first into one mix and then into the other so that you have two colours on the brush. Then drag it through the paint already on the surface, depositing the two colours at once and letting them blend with the colours beneath. As you drag the brush down to the horizon, make a slightly wavering stroke to give movement and energy to the clouds.

Technique

6

SCUMBLING

One of the most beautiful effects in oil painting, scumbling involves brushing thin, dry paint over another layer of colour with a rapid scrubbing motion. Because the colour is applied unevenly the underlayer is only partially obscured and shimmers up through the scumble, creating an "optical" colour mix with extraordinary depth and richness. Scumbling also produces a lively, unpredictable texture in which the marks of the brush are evident.

The technique is used to good effect in this painting to capture the shimmer and the reflective quality of a beach at low tide when viewed directly into the setting sun. The artist worked over the whole canvas with thin veils of stiff, chalky paint scumbled and dragged over a red ground. The warm tone of the ground glows up through the overlaid colours, capturing the pearly, luminous quality that is characteristic of early evening light on the coast.

Barry Freeman
Evening Sun, Portugal
41 x 51cm (16 x 20in)

SCUMBLING

A scumble consists of short, scrubby strokes of thin, dry, semi-opaque colour applied loosely over previous layers of the painting. Because the colour is applied unevenly the underlayer is only partially obscured and shimmers up through the scumble. The interaction between the two layers creates a pleasing effect – the colours mix optically and have more resonance.

Scumbling is also a good way to modify an exisiting colour. A red that is too strident can be subtly "knocked back" by scumbling over it with a cool green, and vice versa. Similarly, passages that have become too "jumpy" and fragmented can be softened and unified by working over them with scumbled colour.

Use stiff bristle or synthetic brushes for scumbling. Pick up some paint on your brush, then flick it across a rag to remove excess moisture. Lightly scrub the paint on with free, vigorous strokes, leaving the brushmarks. The aim is to produce a semi-transparent overlayer, like a haze of smoke, through which the underlayers can be glimpsed. The paint can be worked in various directions. You can also scumble with a rag or a painting knife.

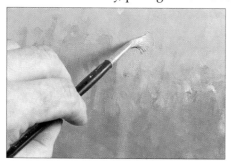

It is important to build up scumbles thinly, in gradual stages. If the paint is applied too heavily, the hazy, veil-like effect will be lost.

EVENING SUN, PORTUGAL

1

Prepare your board by tinting it with a thin, turpsy wash consisting of roughly 70% cadmium red and 30% cerulean. Apply this with a small decorating brush, then wipe over the wet paint with a clean rag to unify the surface. Leave to dry overnight.

Sketch in the main elements of the composition with a small round soft-hair brush, using varied tones of French ultramarine and cadmium red. Indicate the figures with brief, sketchy marks at this stage.

Materials and Equipment

- SHEET OF PRIMED MDF BOARD
- OIL COLOURS: CADMIUM RED, ROSE MADDER, ALIZARIN CRIMSON, CADMIUM LEMON, CADMIUM YELLOW, FRENCH ULTRAMARINE, COBALT BLUE, CERULEAN AND TITANIUM WHITE
- SMALL ROUND SOFT-HAIR BRUSH • MEDIUM ROUND SYNTHETIC BRUSH • SMALL DECORATING BRUSH • LINT-FREE RAG • DISTILLED TURPENTINE
- PURE LINSEED OIL

2

Mix the paint with a little oil-painting medium to give it more body. Don't add too much though – paint for scumbling should be fairly "dry" in consistency. Block in the sky using titanium white "dirtied" with small amounts of cadmium red, cobalt blue and a touch of cadmium yellow. Apply the scumbling paint with lively strokes worked in different directions, using a medium-size, round synthetic brush.

3

Now darken the mixture with more cadmium red and a touch of alizarin crimson and start to paint the sand in the foreground. Apply the paint with loose, scrubby strokes, letting plenty of the warm red of the tinted ground to show through. Modulate the tone and temperature of the sand colour as you work, adding more cobalt to cool the mix, or more cadmium yellow to warm it.

4

Add French ultramarine, plus more cadmium red and cadmium yellow to the mix on the palette to make a dark grey. Paint the cliffs in the background, again modulating the colour from warm to cool by adding more blue or more yellow to the basic mix. Work your brush in different directions to suggest the craggy surface of the cliffs.

5

Lighten the grey mixture with more cobalt blue and titanium white to make a cooler, lighter grey for the headland glimpsed on the right, in the far distance. Now lighten the mix even more, adding plenty of white plus hints of rose madder and cadmium yellow to make a silvery grey. Use this to paint the sea and the rock pool in the foreground, scumbling the paint on loosely with small brushmarks worked in horizontal and vertical directions. Where the shallow water meets the sand, use a thirsty brush and dryish paint, dragging it lightly across so that the strokes break up on the rough surface of the canvas.

6

Mix a soft, neutral tint of cadmium red, cadmium lemon, a little cobalt blue and lots of titanium white. Apply this with lightly scumbled strokes to soften the edge where the water and sand meet and link them naturally together. Then mix varied amounts of cobalt blue, cadmium red and white and paint the cast shadow in the foreground and the rock on the right, letting flecks of the toned ground show through the scumbled strokes.

7

Build up more colour on the cliffs, mixing varied tones of ultramarine, cadmium red and touches of cadmium yellow and white for the dark cliff on the left. Work over the lighter cliffs with varied tones of rose madder, cobalt blue and cadmium yellow mixed in varied proportions. Scuff the paint on lightly so that some of the pink ground glows through and lends a luminosity to the colours.

8

Switch to a small round soft-hair brush and define the figures on the beach using a soft, bluish grey mixed from ultramarine, rose madder and a bit of cadmium yellow. Use the tip of the brush to suggest tiny figures in the distance, beneath the cliffs. The figures should not be too dark as the evening light is soft and hazy.

9

Avoid defining the figures too sharply and making them appear wooden and "pasted on" to the picture. Here the artist has "lost" edges on the figures by smudging the paint. By lightly dragging the colour down from the base of each figure, he also suggests their reflections on the wet sand.

10

Stand back from your painting – or even take a break from it – so you can assess any modifications that need to be made before continuing. Here, for example, the artist realized that the figures form a straight line going into the distance, so he added two more figures, a little to the right, to break the monotony. He also altered the shape of one of the figures, which was too heavy and square. Finally, he warmed the colour of the distant figures with a mix of cadmium red and cobalt blue, and added highlights using white mixed with cobalt blue and a little alizarin.

11

Build up the tones on the sand with varied mixes of white, cadmium lemon, cadmium yellow and a hint of alizarin. Then paint the seaweed-covered rocks in the foreground using scumbled strokes. Start with a violet mix of cadmium red and cobalt blue, then mix cobalt, cadmium yellow and a little cadmium red for the seaweed. Add French ultramarine to the mix for the darker greens, and more yellow and white for the lighter greens on the top of the rock. Lighten the mixes with white to paint the rocks and seaweed in the background.

12

Mix a warm grey with cobalt blue, white and a touch of alizarin and use this to grey down the water in the rock pool. Darken the mix and suggest the figure's reflection in the water. Then mix cadmium red, cadmium yellow and a touch of cobalt and scumble this over the sand in the immediate foreground to deepen its tone and bring it forward.

13

Step back and assess your painting once more, and make any final adjustments to the tones and colours. Use a small round brush to scumble on the sparkling highlights on the water using white tinted with a hint of rose madder and ultramarine. To complete the painting, mix white with cadmium red and yellow and add tiny highlights on the shoulders of some of the background figures lit by the setting sun.

Technique

7

DEVELOPING THE PAINTING

No area of this painting is flat or monotonous – all the tones and colours have been built up with an intricate network of small, separate brushstrokes reminiscent of the French Impressionist painters. The artist developed all areas of the composition at the same rate, moving from one part of the painting to another. Inevitably colour is picked up on the brush and taken from one area to another and these recurring colour notes give the painting an underlying coherence that pulls otherwise disparate elements together and results in a pleasing whole.

When tackling a complex subject such as this, it is good to keep in mind the advice of Cézanne: "Start with a broom and end with a needle." Begin by blocking in the broad areas, then attend to the intermediate shapes and tones, and finally, apply the details and finishing touches.

Derek Daniells
Gondolas, Venice
56 x 46cm (22 x 18in)

DEVELOPING THE PAINTING

A mistake that is sometimes made by inexperienced painters is to work on one small area of a painting until it is "finished", and then to move on to the next section. This technique can result in a confused and disjointed image because each area of tone and colour is unrelated to the neighbouring sections of the work.

Instead of working in piecemeal fashion, try to work over all areas of the canvas simultaneously, moving from foreground to background and letting the composition weave itself into a whole. The image should emerge gradually, rather like a photograph in a developing tray. Keep your eyes moving around the subject, looking for the way tones, colours and shapes relate to each other and making necessary adjust-

ments as you go. You will need to do this because the tones and colours you apply to your canvas will not work in isolation – they will all be influenced by the tones and colours surrounding them. For example, a tone that appears dark on its own will take on a much lighter appearance when it is surrounded by darker tones. Painting is a continuous process of balancing, judging, altering and refining – which is what makes it so totally absorbing.

By building up the tones and colours gradually you will also avoid over-working the surface and churning up the paint, so that when you come to paint in the detail with linear marks and thicker colour towards the final painting of the picture, the colours will remain fresh and the brushstrokes distinct.

GONDOLAS, VENICE

1
Before starting to paint, tone the ground with a thin wash of yellow ochre. Leave to dry for 24 hours, then mix a thin wash of Prussian blue and a little cobalt violet and apply this loosely so that the yellow underlayer gleams up through the blue, creating a lively base colour for the painting. Leave to dry for 24 hours, then mix titanium white and cobalt blue and draw the main elements of the composition with a small round soft-hair brush.

Materials and Equipment

- SHEET OF CANVAS OR BOARD
- OIL COLOURS: CADMIUM RED, YELLOW OCHRE, CADMIUM YELLOW, NAPLES YELLOW, LEMON YELLOW, VIRIDIAN, CERULEAN, PRUSSIAN BLUE, COBALT VIOLET, COBALT BLUE AND TITANIUM WHITE • LARGE FILBERT BRISTLE BRUSH • SMALL ROUND SOFT-HAIR BRUSH
- TURPENTINE • ALKYD MEDIUM

2

Start to block in the main colours using thin paint diluted with turpentine. Mix cerulean, cadmium yellow, yellow ochre and a touch of white and rough in the overhanging vine using a large filbert brush. Vary the proportions of the colours to give variety to the greens. Paint the pink awning with cadmium red, cobalt violet and white; for the blue awning use cerulean and white; add more yellow to the foliage mixture for the green awning. Mix a soft creamy colour from cadmium red, yellow ochre and white and scumble this thinly over the buildings and the steps leading down into the water.

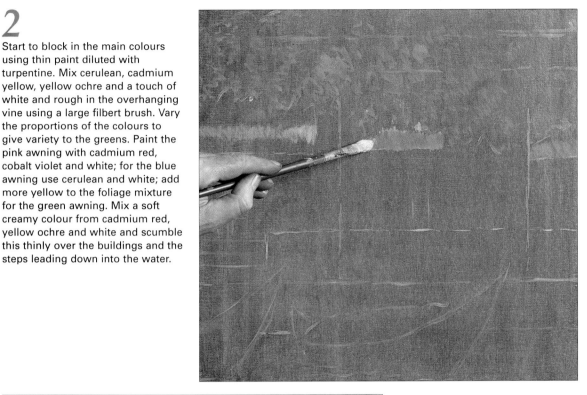

3

Use a small filbert brush to build up tone and texture in the foliage with tiny curved strokes. Mix viridian, Prussian blue and yellow ochre for the darker greens and cerulean, yellow ochre and a touch of cadmium yellow for the lighter greens. Paint the wooden posts with yellow ochre and violet. Mix viridian, cerulean and white and paint the railings of the green balustrade. Then mix a pinkish brown from cadmium red, violet, white and a little cadmium yellow and scumble this over parts of the buildings to give an impression of light and shadow. Work the same colour into the spaces between the railings on the balustrade.

4

Paint the tarpaulin covers on the gondolas with viridian, cerulean and a little white. Now start to paint the water using a small round soft-hair brush to apply small flecks and dashes of broken colour, allowing the dark ground colour to show through. Mix cobalt violet and white for the dark reflections of the gondolas. Then apply loosely spaced strokes of viridian and white over the rest of the water interspersed with soft pinks, yellows and oranges mixed from varying proportions of Naples yellow, cadmium red, yellow ochre and white.

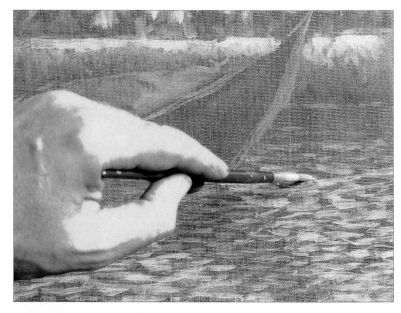

5

Use a network of tiny strokes and dabs of colour to create a shimmering surface that suggests the flickering quality of the light.

6

Don't work on one area in isolation but add touches of colour over the whole image. Scumble greens onto the vine, then add strokes of cadmium red mixed with varying amounts of yellow ochre and white to the buildings. Mix yellow ochre, cadmium red, cobalt violet and a hint of white for the shadow beneath the green awning. Indicate the doors and windows with cerulean and white, and the poles supporting the vine with viridian and white.

7

Paint the boat hulls with Prussian blue, viridian and a little white, adding more Prussian blue for the shadowed parts. Indicate the shadowy folds on the tarpaulins with Prussian blue, cerulean and white. Lighten the tone of the balustrade with tiny, broken strokes, using varied mixes of viridian, white and yellow ochre. Continue building up the highlights and reflections in the water with broken strokes of pink, green, violet and soft yellow. Mix cadmium red, cadmium yellow and white for the pinks; viridian, lemon yellow and white for the pale greens; yellow ochre and white for the creams, and cobalt violet and white for the violets.

8

Continue working all over the canvas, gradually modifying the colours you have put down to bring the picture into focus. Use a small round brush to complete the foliage, defining the darks with Prussian blue, yellow ochre and a touch of violet and the lights with yellow ochre, cerulean, white and a touch of viridian. Build up the colours in the water, and don't forget to define the reflections of the boats and the mooring poles.

Technique

8

KNIFE PAINTING

Essentially, the painting knife is a miniature "trowel" and may be used alone, or in conjunction with brush painting, to apply oil paint to the canvas in a direct and spontaneous manner. Knife painting is ideal for the artist who enjoys the tactile sensation of applying thick, buttery paint to the canvas, moving it around and partially scraping it off with the edge of the blade, or scratching into the wet paint to suggest details and texture.

This striking composition was executed entirely with a painting knife, the colours applied in a thick impasto over a thin underpainting. The ridged texture of the paint stands out in relief and casts tiny shadows that enhance the texture of the grasses and thistles and give a suggestion of movement and changing light.

The artist chose a high viewpoint, looking out over a valley, but crouched low so that the flowers and grasses dwarf the landscape behind. Such an exciting contrast of scale adds greatly to the impact of the picture.

Brian Bennett
Sowthistles and Grasses
41 x 56cm (16 x 22in)

KNIFE PAINTING

Knife painting is a versatile and expressive method of building up layers of thick impasto to create a richly textured paint surface.

Painting knives are not the same as palette knives, which have a straight handle and a long straight blade and are used for mixing paint on the palette and for cleaning up. A painting knife has a very springy, responsive blade and a cranked handle to prevent the knuckles accidentally brushing against the canvas when applying the paint. Knives are available in different sizes and in trowel, diamond and elliptical shapes, for creating a range of textures and effects.

Painting with a knife is initially trickier than painting with a brush, so it is wise to practise until you get the feel of it. You can apply the paint in broad sweeps with the flat of the knife, or use the tip to get sharp, angular marks. "Printing" with the edge of the blade produces fine linear marks, useful, for example, when painting the rigging on boats. You can also skim paint off the canvas with the edge of the blade to leave a translucent stain of colour.

Painting knives encourage a lively and impressionistic treatment, yet are capable of achieving fine detail.

SOWTHISTLES AND GRASSES

1

Mix a brownish grey from cobalt blue, Vandyke brown and titanium white and dilute to a thin consistency with oil-painting medium. Use this to plot in the main compositional lines and the broad areas of light and dark, scrubbing the paint on quite dryly with a large filbert bristle brush.

Materials and Equipment

• SHEET OF CANVAS OR CANVAS BOARD • OIL COLOURS: ALIZARIN CRIMSON, FLESH TINT, YELLOW OCHRE, CHROME YELLOW, LEMON YELLOW, CADMIUM YELLOW PALE, WINSOR GREEN, FRENCH ULTRAMARINE, COBALT BLUE, INDIGO, VANDYKE BROWN AND TITANIUM WHITE • LARGE FILBERT BRISTLE BRUSH • TROWEL-SHAPED PAINTING KNIFE
• REFINED LINSEED OIL
• DISTILLED TURPENTINE

2

Still using the brush, build up an underpainting in thin colour using broad, sweeping strokes. Block in the sky with a pale mix of white, indigo and a little alizarin crimson. Then establish the light and dark tones in the landscape, mixing warm and cool greens from varied proportions of indigo, yellow ochre, chrome yellow and touches of the colours already mixed on your palette.

3

Start to overpaint with the knife, using thicker colour mixed with a little medium. Mix French ultramarine, white and a little alizarin for the upper sky, changing from ultramarine to cooler cobalt blue as you work downwards. Introduce warmer tints (flesh tint, yellow ochre and white) near the horizon. Mix indigo, ultramarine, white and a touch of Vandyke brown for the dark clouds. Touch the colour on with the edge of the blade and then smooth it out with the flat, working the colours into each other, wet-in-wet.

4

Continue building up the massed heaps of storm cloud with thick, creamy paint. For the warmer tops of the clouds, mix yellow ochre, flesh tint and white, softly blending the colour into the grey beneath. Use the back of the knife to drag colour down from the base of the clouds to give the impression of distant rain. This also creates subtle rhythms that lead the eye down to the landscape.

5

Add the fields in the far distance by applying narrow bands of thick paint. For the darks, mix indigo, alizarin and a little white; for the lights, mix cadmium yellow pale, chrome yellow and a little white warmed with yellow ochre in places. Then draw the edge of the knife through the paint to create a series of delicate lines and ridges suggesting fields and hedgerows in the background.

6

Here you can see how the ridges in the paint reflect the topography of the distant landscape, the variations in colour and tone suggesting patches of light and shadow cast by the cloudy sky. Now paint the bank of hawthorn trees in the middle distance, starting with an underlayer of indigo, alizarin and Winsor green applied with slanted strokes. Work over this with warm greens mixed from varying proportions of yellow ochre, chrome yellow, indigo and Winsor green, with the knife strokes following the forms of the trees.

7

Define the curve of the dirt track leading into the distance with Vandyke brown, yellow ochre and white mixed in varying proportions to create a variety of warm lights and cooler darks. Notice how the curve of the track and the shapes of the clouds both help to lead the eye into the picture.

8

On your palette, mix a dark brown from yellow ochre, Vandyke brown and a touch of flesh tint, and a warm yellow from yellow ochre, white and a little lemon yellow. Pick up some dark brown on the edge of the knife and use it to "draw" a series of fine, gently curved lines suggesting stalks and grasses, altering the pressure on the knife as you drag it downwards. Now go over the lines with the yellow mixture; this creates a convincing three-dimensional impression, giving the stalks a lit side and a shadowy side.

9

Paint the seed heads using delicate upward flicks with the tip of the knife. Again, apply the dark brown first and then add the yellow for the highlights. Paint the grasses dark against the light parts of the sky, and vice versa; this tonal contrast – called "counterchange" – not only creates visual interest but also helps to create space and distance between the foreground and the background.

10

Continue painting the stalks and grasses. Avoid creating a "barrier" across the picture by making some grasses taller than others and by varying the density of the clumps so that they appear natural. The dirt track on the left is a useful device, creating a break in the foreground that invites the viewer into the picture. Mix various warm and cool greens from yellow ochre, indigo, Winsor green, chrome yellow and white and apply these with broad knife strokes in the foreground.

11

Combine yellow ochre, white and a little lemon yellow and fill in some shorter grasses in the immediate foreground of the painting. Merge the bases of the stems into the greens applied in step 10 so that they appear to emerge naturally from the ground. This detail clearly shows the three-dimensional effect of the thick, raised knife marks. You can almost hear the dry grasses rustling in the breeze!

12

Now paint the bright yellow sow thistle flowers using chrome and cadmium yellows "dirtied" with a touch of grey from your palette (first scrape away some of the underlying paint so that the yellow doesn't pick up the blue of the sky). Vary the size, shape and direction of the flower heads – and resist the temptation to put in too many. Suggest some flowers further back amongst the grasses with little touches and smears of paint – don't outline them too clearly otherwise they will jump forward.

13

This close-up reveals how the daisy-like flowers are suggested by applying thick strokes of paint with the tip of the knife, and then feathering them to create ragged edges. Paint the pods under the flowers using warm and cool greens mixed from indigo and chrome yellow. Finish off by painting in the darker centres on some of the flowers with yellow ochre and by touching in one or two white flowers to offset the bright yellows.

Technique

9

BLENDING

Oil paint lends itself readily to the blending technique because its soft, buttery consistency and slow drying time allow it to be extensively manipulated on the canvas.

In this still-life study colours are applied over and into one another while still wet, producing subtle gradations of tone and colour that describe the rounded forms of the jug and lemons and give them solidity and weight. The artist was careful, however, to retain the liveliness of the brushmarks, as overblending can make the surface look monotonous.

The standard oil-painting medium (two-thirds turpentine and one-third linseed oil) will give the paint the right amount of body and fluidity for blending wet-into-wet. However, as you gain more experience you should experiment with different mediums as some may be better suited to your way of working than others. In this instance, the artist has used a medium consisting of equal amounts of linseed oil and dammar varnish plus twice the volume of turpentine. This medium holds the marks of the brush well and gives the paint surface an attractive, matt and airy quality.

~

James Horton
Jug and Lemons
25 x 21cm (10 x 8in)

~

BLENDING TECHNIQUE

Blending is a means of achieving smooth gradations between adjacent tones or colours by brushing them together wet-into-wet. It is used to render soft materials and surface qualities such as fabrics, skin tones, flowers and the reflective surfaces of metal and glass. It can also be used to describe certain atmospheric impressions found in the landscape, such as skies and clouds, fog and mist, and reflections in water.

The techniques of blending colour fall between two extremes. On the one hand you can blend the colour with your brush so smoothly and silkily that the brushstrokes are imperceptible even when viewed close-up. At the other extreme it is possible to knit the colours together roughly so that the brushmarks remain visible at close quarters; when viewed at a distance the colours appear to merge together, yet they retain a lively quality because they are only partially blended.

Any type of brush can be used for blending, depending on your style of painting. Some artists use stiff-bristled brushes so they retain the liveliness of the brushstrokes. Others prefer to use soft-hair brushes to achieve very smooth gradations. Brushes called "fan blenders" – they have long hairs arranged in a fan shape – are specially adapted for smooth blending; work over the edge between two tones or colours using a gentle sweeping motion until a smooth, imperceptible blend is achieved.

JUG AND LEMONS

Left: The items in this still life were chosen for their gently rounded forms, which are ideally suited to the technique of blending colour wet-in-wet. Bright complementary colours – blues and purples, oranges and yellows – enliven the composition.

Materials and Equipment

• SHEET OF PRIMED HARDBOARD OR MDF • OIL COLOURS: ALIZARIN CRIMSON, YELLOW OCHRE, CHROME YELLOW, LEMON YELLOW, CADMIUM ORANGE, VERMILION, TERRE VERTE, FRENCH ULTRAMARINE, COBALT BLUE, BURNT SIENNA, RAW UMBER AND TITANIUM WHITE • 25MM (1IN) DECORATING BRUSH • MEDIUM AND SMALL ROUND BRISTLE BRUSHES • SMALL ROUND SABLE OR SYNTHETIC BRUSH • RIGGER BRUSH • REFINED LINSEED OIL • DISTILLED TURPENTINE • DAMMAR VARNISH

1

Start by tinting the board with a neutral mid-tone to eliminate the stark white of the priming. Mix burnt sienna and a little French ultramarine with lots of turpentine to a thin consistency. Apply this freely across the board with a 25mm (1in) household brush. Leave to dry overnight.

Sketch out the main outlines of the composition using a small round sable or synthetic brush and French ultramarine diluted with turpentine to make it flow easily.

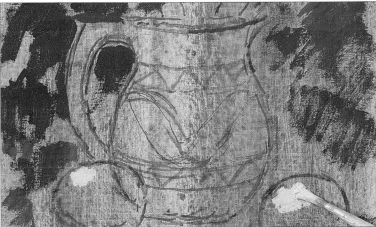

2

It is often a good idea to plot the lightest and darkest tones early on, as they provide a useful reference for the mid-tones. Rough in the darks in the blue backcloth with a mixture of ultramarine, alizarin crimson and titanium white applied with a medium round bristle brush. Scrub the paint on with loose, open strokes that allow the tinted ground to show through. Apply dabs of neat chrome yellow on the tops of the lemons to establish the lightest tones in the image.

3

Block in the shadows on the lemons with a mix of lemon yellow, ultramarine and a drop of cadmium orange. Start to work on the jug, establishing the broad tones of light and shade. For the lighter tone, mix white with a touch of cadmium orange; for the shadow side, mix a warm grey from yellow ochre, ultramarine, white and terre verte. Roughly block in the tones. Make no attempt to blend at this stage.

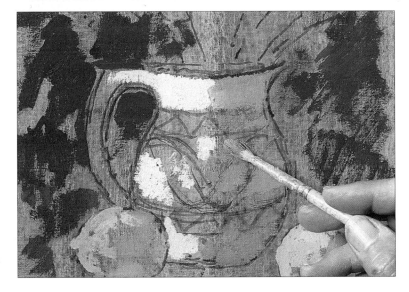

4

Use the dark blue mixed in step 2 to put a shadow under the jug and lemons to give them a feeling of solidity and weight. Then add more white to the mix and rough in the lighter blue of the cloth in the foreground. Switch to a smaller round bristle brush to paint the decorative pattern on the jug. For the dark blues, mix ultramarine, cobalt blue and alizarin crimson. For the greenish blues mix ultramarine, cobalt and lemon yellow. And for the greens mix ultramarine and lemon yellow. Remember to darken the tone of each colour as the jug turns into shadow, graduating the tones by blending them wet-in-wet.

5

Paint the brown patterns on the jug with burnt sienna and white. Then start to work on the flowers, mixing cadmium orange, vermilion and white for the carnations, and ultramarine, lemon yellow and white for the foliage. Vary the proportions of the colours used in each mix to create a range of warms and cools and lights and darks.

6

Define the curve of the top of the jug and the spout with further gradations of tone. The basic mix is raw umber, yellow ochre and white, with more white added for the lightest tone at the front, more raw umber for the darkest tone, and a touch of cadmium orange added for the darker, warmer tone in between.

7

Now use the medium round bristle brush to describe the light folds in the backcloth, using a mixture of ultramarine, alizarin crimson and white. Vary the tones by adding more white in the lighter folds.

Use the small round bristle brush to develop the forms of the flowers, adding touches of vermilion to define the petals. Paint some of the statice flowers with a mix of ultramarine and alizarin, adding a hint of white in the lighter areas. Mix white with a touch of cadmium orange to add warm tints to the lit side of the jug and its handle.

8

Define the rounded forms of the lemons with tonal gradations from light to dark. Using the medium round brush, work over the highlights with a mix of chrome yellow and white, then add a little raw umber to the mix for the mid-tones. Finally, add more raw umber and a little cadmium orange for the warm shadows at the base of the lemons. Use thick, juicy paint and lively brushmarks that follow the forms of the fruits, blending the tones together where they meet to define the different planes.

9

Feather over the different tones on the jug with a dry brush to soften them. Give definition to the carnations at the front, adding swirls of vermilion and picking out the light petals with vermilion, lemon yellow and white. Add more of the purple statice flowers using ultramarine, alizarin and white.

Stand back and decide on any final adjustments. Add pale highlights along the tops of the lemons using white and a little lemon yellow. Use a rigger brush to redefine any edges that have become ragged, such as on the handle of the jug.

Technique
10

UNDERPAINTING

Many painters like to start a complex oil painting by brushing in the broad areas of the composition in thin colour in order to help them organize the picture in terms of shapes and tones.

Making an underpainting is, in effect, a way of "starting before you've begun". The intimidating white of the canvas is quickly covered, and at a very early stage the picture already reads as a whole. The underpainting may be completely covered as the picture is built up, or it can play an active role in the final painting if parts of it are left visible. This creates a pleasing contrast between thin and thick applications of paint, as well as breathing air into the painting and injecting a lively, working feel.

Underpainting is traditionally done in a monochrome grey or earth colour, which acts as a guide for the light and dark tones in the image. In this painting, however, the artist chose to underpaint in light colours approximating those of the subject. Thus the succeeding colours, as well as tones, are more easily judged against the underpainting.

Ted Gould
Coffee and Croissant
36 x 46cm (14 x 18in)

UNDERPAINTING

The traditional way of starting an oil painting is to block in the broad shapes and masses with thin paint before adding the details and surface colour. The underpainting gives you the opportunity to organize the composition and the distribution of light and dark values at the outset, and to resolve any problems before starting to paint. Because the paint is thin, corrections are easily made at this stage by wiping with a rag.

The result is a practical division of labour; once the underpainting is complete you can concentrate on colour and detail, confident that the composition and tonal values are sound.

Traditionally, neutral greys, blues or earth colours are used to underpaint. The darks and mid-tones are established with tones of one colour, leaving the white or tinted canvas to act as the highlights. Underpainting may also be done in colours that either complement or contrast with the overall colour values of the subject. For example, an underpainting in warm browns or reds will give resonance to the cool greens of a landscape. The underpainting can also be laid in several colours that relate to those used in the final painting.

Colours for underpainting should be thinly diluted with turpentine or white (mineral) spirit. The underpainting must also be thoroughly dry before you start the overpainting. To save time, you can underpaint with acrylic colours (thinly diluted with water) and then overpaint in oils. Acrylics dry within minutes, allowing you to apply the next layer in oil almost immediately.

COFFEE AND CROISSANT

Left: A pretty and informal breakfast setting is the subject of this still life. Although the objects appear casually arranged, they are in fact carefully composed to create a strong, cohesive group.

Materials and Equipment

• SHEET OF CANVAS OR BOARD
• ACRYLIC COLOURS: BRIGHT RED, CRIMSON, LEMON YELLOW YELLOW OCHRE, BRIGHT GREEN, FRENCH ULTRAMARINE AND BURNT SIENNA • OIL COLOURS: INDIAN RED, VENETIAN RED, SCARLET LAKE, ALIZARIN CRIMSON, YELLOW OCHRE, WINSOR YELLOW, WINSOR GREEN, FRENCH ULTRAMARINE AND TITANIUM WHITE • SMALL ROUND SYNTHETIC BRUSH
• SMALL, MEDIUM AND LARGE FLAT BRISTLE BRUSHES
• TURPENTINE • LINSEED OIL
• JAR OF WATER

1

Start by drawing the main outlines using acrylics. Mix yellow ochre with a touch of French ultramarine and dilute with water to a thin consistency. Sketch loosely with a small round synthetic brush. Horizontal and vertical axes lines will help you to draw the round and elliptical shapes accurately. Leave to dry – this will take only a few minutes.

2

Now establish the underpainting, again using fast-drying acrylic paints. Mix a thin, watery wash of yellow ochre warmed with a little burnt sienna, and use a large flat synthetic brush to loosely block in the background. Darken the mix with ultramarine and touch in the coffee in the mug using a medium-sized flat brush. Mix yellow ochre and bright red for the orange, then add a touch of burnt sienna to the mix and block in the split croissant and the knife blade. Work thinly and rapidly, not worrying about details at this stage.

3

Continue underpainting with colours approximating those of the actual objects. Use very thinly diluted crimson for the napkin, darkened with ultramarine for the shadows and creases. Block in the geranium flowers with crimson mixed with lemon yellow for the warmer reds and ultramarine for the cooler, darker reds. Use bright green for the geranium leaves, adding lemon yellow for the warmer greens and ultramarine for the cooler greens. Paint the blue cockerel pattern on the mug with ultramarine, then add burnt sienna for the cast shadows.

4

Once the acrylic underpainting is dry you can start to overpaint in oils, thinning the colours with turpentine and linseed oil medium. First, block in the background with loosely mixed Indian red, yellow ochre, Winsor yellow and titanium white. Use a large flat bristle brush and sweep the paint on quite vigorously, working the brush in different directions and letting the marks of the brush show. Paint up to the still-life forms, then cut into them to begin to define them.

5

Use a medium-sized flat brush to define the orange with Winsor yellow and Indian red, adding more yellow for the light tones on top and more red for the shadows. For the deeper shadow near the base, darken with a little alizarin. Mix yellow ochre, white and a touch of ultramarine for the knife handle. Paint the shadows on the table with a mix of yellow ochre, Indian red and ultramarine. Define the croissant halves using Indian red broken with yellow ochre, Winsor yellow and white. Add more Indian red for the crusty tops. Follow the forms with your brushstrokes.

6

Paint the coffee in the mug with a mix of Indian red, ultramarine and yellow ochre. Mix a warm grey from ultramarine, yellow ochre and a touch of Indian red and put in the shadows on the plate and the blade of the knife. Define the flower jug with pale greys mixed from ultramarine, yellow ochre, a touch of Indian red and plenty of white. Create different subtle tones, adding more blue for the shadows on the jug. Mix alizarin and Winsor yellow and block in the geraniums with strokes in different directions. Add ultramarine for darker reds.

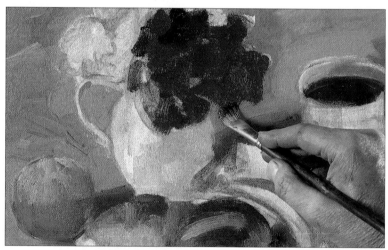

7

Now work on the pink napkin, first blocking in the local colour with a medium-toned mix of alizarin crimson, white and a touch of ultramarine. Then define the creases and folds with thick, creamy paint applied with a small flat brush. Mix alizarin crimson and ultramarine for the shadowy folds, and white with a touch of alizarin for the highlights along the tops of the folds.

8

Return to the geranium flowers and start to define the petals with short strokes of thick, juicy paint, letting the individual brushstrokes form the shapes of the petals. Mix some scarlet lake and a touch of titanium white for the lightest petals, and alizarin crimson and ultramarine for the darker, cooler petals. Add touches of Venetian red for the warm shadows between the blooms.

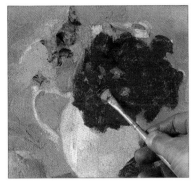

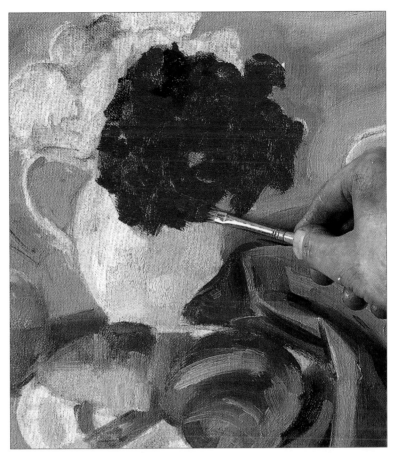

9

Now paint the geranium leaves in the same way, pivoting from the wrist to follow their curved forms with blocks of colour and tone. Use pure Winsor green for the darkest tones, adding Winsor yellow for the bright greens and a touch of yellow ochre for the warm mid-tones. Cut into the flowers with small strokes of green to indicate the gaps between the blooms.

10

Refine the tones on the jug and plate with smooth strokes of white, broken with hints of alizarin and ultramarine blended into the greys applied earlier. Suggest the napkin's reflection on the jug with a hint of alizarin and white. Define the blue and white pattern on the coffee mug with ultramarine and white.

11

Mix ultramarine with a hint of Indian red and paint the decorative blue pattern on the jug and plate with the tip of a small round soft-hair brush. Paint the reflections on the knife blade with strokes of ultramarine, Indian red and yellow ochre. Switch to a small flat bristle brush and suggest the grain of the wooden table with loose drybrush strokes of white and yellow ochre mixed with ultramarine and Indian red. Enrich the colours on the croissant with thick strokes of Indian red and Winsor yellow. Then use white greyed with hints of ultramarine and Indian red to suggest the sugar-frosting on the top of the croissant with feathery strokes of thick paint applied with a thirsty brush.

12

Develop light and shade on the orange with thickly impasted strokes of alizarin crimson, Winsor yellow, white and a touch of scarlet lake, with more yellow ochre for the greenish shadow on the right. Paint the dimple with ultramarine and Indian red, and add the bright highlights with thick dabs of pure white. Mix ultramarine, Indian red and yellow ochre for the dark shadows on the surface of the coffee. Finally, add more texture and movement in the background with loose mixtures of Indian red, yellow ochre, Winsor yellow and white applied with vigorous strokes of creamy paint.

Suppliers

United Kingdom

Copystat Cardiff Ltd
44 Charles Street
Cardiff CF1 4EE
Tel: 01222 344422
Tel: 01222 566136 (mail order)
(general art suppliers)

Daler Rowney Ltd
12 Percy Street
London W1A 9BP
Tel: 0171 636 8241
(painting and drawing materials)

John Mathieson & Co
48 Frederick Street
Edinburgh EH2 1HG
Tel: 0131 225 6798
(general art supplies)

L. Cornelissen & Son Ltd
105 Great Russell Street
London WC1B 3LA
Tel: 0171 636 1045
(general art supplies)

Winsor & Newton
51 Rathbone Place
London W1P 1AB
Tel: 0171 636 4231
(painting and drawing materials)

South Africa

Art & Craft & Hobbies
72 Hibernia Street
P. O. Box 9635
George 6530
Tel: (0441) 74 1337
(Also offers all-hours nationwide
mail-order service)

Art Supplies
16 Ameshof Street
Braamfontein
Gauteng
Tel: (011) 339 2268

The Artist's Friend
Russel House, 41 Sir Lowry Road
Cape Town
Tel: (021) 45 4027 Fax: (021) 461 2901

Herbert Evans Art Shop
Cnr Nugget and Jeppe Streets
Johannesburg
Tel: (011) 402 2040

In-Fin-Art
9 Wolfe Street
Wynberg Cape Town
Tel: (021) 761 2816 Fax: (021) 761 1884

PW Story
18 Foundry Lane
Durban
Tel: (031) 306 1224

Shop 148
The Pavilion
Westville
Tel: (031) 265 0250

Australia

Art Stretchers Co Pty Ltd
188 Morphett Street
Adelaide, South Australia 5000
Tel: (08) 212 2711

Artiscare
101 York Street
South Melbourne, Victoria 33205
Tel: (03) 9699 6188

Creative Hot Shop
96b Beaufort Street
Perth, Western Australia 6000
Tel: (08) 328 5437

Eckersley's
Cnr Edward and Mary Streets
Brisbane, Queensland 4000
Tel: (07) 3221 4866

Oxford Art Supplies
221–223 Oxford Street
Darlinghurst NSW 2010
Tel: (02) 360 4066

New Zealand

Draw-Art Supplies Ltd
5 Mahunga Drive
Mangere
Tel: (09) 636 4862

The French Art Shop
51 Ponsonby Road
Ponsonby
Tel: (09) 379 4976

Gordon Harris
Art & Drawing Office Supplies
4 Gillies Avenue
Newmarket
Tel: (09) 520 4466

Studio Art Supplies (Parnell) Ltd
225 Parnell Road
Parnell
Tel: (09) 377 0302

Takapuna Art Supplies
18 Northcroft Street
Takapuna
Tel: (09) 489 7213

United States

Art Supply Warehouse
360 Main Avenue
Norwalk
CT 06851
Tel: (800) 243 5038
(general art supplies – mail order)

Creative Materials Catalog
P. O. Box 1267
Gatesburg
IL 61401
Tel: (800) 447 8192
(general art supplies – mail order)

Hofcraft
P. O. Box 1791
Grand Rapids
MI 49501
Tel: (800) 435 7554
(general art supplies – mail order)

Pearl Paints
308 Canal Street
New York
NY 10013 2572
Tel: (800) 415 7327
(general art supplies – mail order)

INDEX

Above Beck Hole, Near Whitby 23
Accessories 15
Acrylic paints 39, 90
Acrylic primer 16, 39
Acrylic texture paste 13, 16
Alla prima 27–31, 33, 46
Apollo 24
Arnolfini Marriage, The 7
Artists' colours 10, 12
Autumn Window 20, 21

Basic techniques 16–19
Bathers on the Strand 24
Bennett, Brian 75
Blending 83–7
Boards 14, 15, 16
Bouquet and Fruit 44–5, 47-51
Bright brushes 14
Bristle brushes 13, 14, 34
Brushes 12, 13, 14
   for blending 12, 14, 84
   cleaning and care 19
   experimenting with 54
   for impasto 14, 34
   see also individually by type eg Sable brushes
Brushwork, expressive 53–9

Canvas 14, 15, 16
Carr, David 27, 53
Cézanne, Paul 69
Chamberlain, Trevor 22
Coffee and Croissant 88–94
Constable, John 8, 28
Corot, Jean-Baptiste-Camille 28
Correcting errors 18–19
Cotton canvas 15
Cracking 45, 46
Curtis, David 23

Dali, Salvador 9
Dammar varnish 12, 14
Daniells, Derek 33, 69
Denahy, John 24
Developing the painting 69–73
Diluents 10, 12, 14
   uses 34, 40, 45, 46
Dippers 12, 15
Disposable palettes 12, 15
Drying times
   acrylic paints 39, 90
   oil paints 46
Dusk San Mario 25

Easton, Timothy 21
Errors, correcting 18–19
Evening Sun, Portugal 60–7
Expressive brushwork 53–9
Eyck, Jan van 7

Fan blender brushes 12, 14, 84
"Fat over lean" 45–51
Fat paint 45, 46
Filbert brushes 12, 14

Flat brushes 12, 14
Freeman, Barry 23, 61
French Impressionists 9, 28
French Interior 38–43
Full Summer 25

Gesso primer 13, 16
Glue size 16
Gogh, Vincent Willem van 34
Gondolas, Venice 68–73
Gould, Ted 89
Grades of paint 10
Graham, Peter 25, 45
Grain Stacks, End of Summer 9
Grounds 16-17, 39–43

Hardboard 15, 16
Hélèna Fourment with a Carriage 8
Hog bristle brushes 13, 14
Horton, James 22, 25, 39, 83
Household decorating brushes 13, 16

Impasto 33–7, 75
Impressionists 9, 28, 69
Improvised palettes 15

Jug and Lemons 82–7

Keys and stretchers 13, 15
Knife painting 75–81
Knives
   painting 13, 15, 34, 76
   palette 13, 15, 18, 76

Lean paint 45, 46
Linen canvas 15
Linseed oil 12, 14

Mahl sticks 12, 15
Materials and equipment 10–15
   see also individually by type eg Brushes
Mediums 10, 14
   uses 34, 83
Monastery, Tuscany 32–7
Monet, Claude 8, 9

Oil painting, history and development 7–9
Oil paints 10, 11, 12, 13
   development by van Eyck 7
   drying times 46
   fat and lean 45, 46
   "orange juice" consistency 40, 45
   suggested palette 11, 17
Oil sketching paper 15
"Orange juice" paint consistency 40, 45
Orange Sunshade 23

Painting knives 13, 15, 34, 76
Paintings, developing 69–73
Paints *see* Acrylic paints; Oil paints
Palette (colour range), suggested 11, 17
Palette knives 13, 15, 18, 76
Palettes (artists' equipment) 12, 15

how to hold 18
   layout of paints 17–18
Paper, oil sketching 15
Pissarro, Camille 9
Pollock, Paul Jackson 9
Priming and primers 13, 15, 16, 39

Rabbit-skin size 13
Rembrandt Harmenszoon van Rijn 6, 7, 8, 34
Renoir, Pierre-Auguste 9
Round brushes 12, 14
Rubens, Peter Paul 8

Sable brushes 12, 14
Scaling up 19
Scumbling 61–7
Self-Portrait at the Easel 6, 7
Shapes and sizes, brushes 12, 13, 14
Size, glue or rabbit-skin 13, 16
Sketching paper, oil 15
Sowthistles and Grasses 74–81
Squaring up 19
Storm Approaching 52–9
Stretchers and keys 13, 15
Students' colours 10, 13
Studio palettes 12, 15
Suppliers 95
Supports 14, 15, 16
Surrealists 9
Synthetic brushes 12, 14

Tarrant, Olwen 24
Texture paste 13, 16
Thumbhole palettes 12, 15
Titian 8
Toned grounds 16–17, 39–43
Tonking 18–19
Tonks, Henry 19
Tulips in the Sun 22
Turner, Joseph Mallord William 8
Turpentine 10, 12, 14, 40, 45, 46
Tuscan Landscape 26–31

Underpainting 46, 89–94

Van Eyck *see* Eyck, Jan van
Van Gogh *see* Gogh, Vincent Willem van
Varnishes 12, 13, 14
Varnishing brushes 13
Velázquez, Diego Rodriguez de Silva 8

Washing on the Line 22
White spirit 10, 40, 46
Working "fat over lean" 45–51

PICTURE CREDITS
The author and publishers would like to thank the following for permission to reproduce additional photographs:

Visual Arts Library: pages 6–9

Index compiled by Susan Bosanko